PROMISE DRIFT

THE INVISIBLE GAP BETWEEN WHAT COMPANIES PROMISE AND WHAT CUSTOMERS EXPERIENCE.

ARTURO COTO

PROMISE ALIGNMENT COMPANY

Published by Promise Alignment Company

Cover design by CloverCoto.com

ISBN:

979-8-9952569-0-8 Hardcover

979-8-9952569-1-5 Paperback

979-8-9952569-2-2 Ebook

First Edition

PromiseDrift.com

PromiseAlignment.com

For my Mom - the bravest leader I'll ever know.

For my family - the greatest gift a promise created.

CONTENTS

INTRODUCTION

The Promise Problem

Every business is built on promises.

Some promises are explicit: "We'll deliver on Friday." "This software will automate your workflow." "Your support team responds within 24 hours."

Most promises are invisible—the assumptions customers make about speed, quality, reliability, safety, service, or care.

But all promises, either consciously or unconsciously, become expectations.

And expectations, once formed, are a reality that must be managed.

This is where the customer expectation gap begins.

This is where companies struggle.

Not because they lack talent. Not because they lack passion. Not because they lack vision.

They struggle because the modern business environment, intentionally or not, creates so many more promises than most companies can keep up with. **The result is a strategy execution gap—where what leadership intends and what customers experience are two completely different realities.**

Every day, promises leak into the world through:

- Marketing copy
- Sales calls
- Onboarding flows
- Artificial Intelligence (AI) chatbots
- Outdated documentation
- Legacy websites
- Offshore teams
- Automated emails

- Half-announced roadmap ideas
- Founder enthusiasm
- Employee improvisation

This is **Promise Drift: the gradual misalignment between what your company promises and what it consistently delivers.** It's the root cause of over-promising and under-delivering—but unlike the typical story of a sales rep making reckless commitments, Promise Drift happens systematically across your entire organization. It happens when promises proliferate faster than your organization can manage them—through decentralized messaging, employee improvisation, AI systems generating responses, legacy content that never gets updated, and scaling complexity that fragments communication.

The result: your company makes hundreds of promises it never intended to set, creating a customer expectation gap you can't reliably close. A promise made by marketing contradicts what support can deliver. Your AI chatbot guarantees features that don't exist. Your offshore team follows outdated policies because no one told them things changed. **What started as a strategy execution gap—where vision doesn't translate to reality—becomes a brand promise gap that erodes customer trust.**

Promise Drift isn't caused by bad intentions—it's caused by organizational growth without deliberate promise management. And without a system to align promises across teams, tools, and touch points, the gap between what you say and what you do will only widen.

It's why teams feel overwhelmed.

It's why customers feel misled.

It's why leaders feel like they're fighting fires instead of building momentum.

It's why companies grow messy instead of strong.

Promise Drift is not a flaw. It's gravity. A natural pull that affects all organizations.

But here's the good news: **You can beat it.**

How This Book Will Help

By the time you finish this book, you will have something most leaders never get: a clear, honest picture of every promise your company is making — and a practical system for making sure you can keep them.

That system is called the **Promise Alignment System (PAS)**. It was built for organizations exactly like yours — companies where the gap between what's promised and what's delivered has quietly become a source of stress, churn, and confusion that no one knows how to name, let alone fix.

PAS gives you six tools that work together as one operating system:

- **The Core Promise** — The single outcome your company delivers consistently and confidently. The promise every team protects.
- **The Promise Stack** — A structured view of all promises customers experience — Core, Supporting, Conditional, Experimental, and Legacy. Nothing hidden. Nothing accidental.
- **The Promise Gate** — A decision framework that prevents over-promising: Can we deliver this? Should we? Will we — every time, without heroics?
- **The Alignment Rhythm** — The cadence where promises are reviewed, reinforced, and redirected — before drift causes damage.
- **The Alignment Network** — The humans and systems accountable for keeping promises — not just making them.
- **The Drift Audit** — The process for surfacing every promise you're making, intentionally or not.

You don't need to be in crisis to use this. But if you are in crisis, it will show you why — and exactly what to fix first.

Part 1 follows a leadership team at AxisLine, a fictional company, as they discover the real cost of drift and rebuild their organization around a single, honest promise. The story is intentionally messy. Their AI keeps hallucinating for weeks. Sales rebels. The first attempt at a Stack Review falls apart. Their consultant transitions from daily partner to quarterly advisor, forcing the team to own the system themselves. You'll recognize your company in their story — not because the details will match, but because the feeling will.

Part 2 is your playbook. Each chapter gives you the frameworks, worksheets, and implementation steps to install PAS in your own organization. You can follow it sequentially over 90 days, or go directly to the chapter that addresses your most urgent problem right now.

Here is what changes when you do the work:

Your teams stop improvising. They know exactly what they're authorized to promise, and they stop apologizing for commitments they didn't make.

Your customers stop being surprised. They hear the same clear message from Sales, Support, your website, your AI, and your offshore teams — and that consistency builds the kind of trust that drives renewals, referrals, and retention.

Your leaders make decisions faster, because every decision runs through one question: *Does this protect our Core Promise?* Your AI stops making things up.

Your documentation stops reflecting a company you used to be.

Your metrics — NPS, churn, support volume, onboarding time — start moving in the right direction, not because you worked harder, but because the whole organization is finally pulling in the same direction.

You become a Promise Company. A company that means what it says, delivers what it promises, and grows because of it — not in spite of the chaos.

PAS is simple enough to understand quickly, powerful enough to scale globally, and modern enough to work with AI, offshore teams, and the full complexity of how organizations actually operate today.

That's what this book is for.

PAS Works With, Not Against, Your Existing Frameworks

You don't need to abandon what's already working. PAS enhances the frameworks you're already using:

- **Running Objectives and Key Results (OKRs) or Key Performance Indicators (KPIs)?** PAS ensures the outcomes you're measuring align with the promises you're making. No more hitting targets while losing customer trust.
- **Using Agile or Scrum for your software development?** PAS adds a promise lens to your sprints, making sure what you build matches what customers expect.
- **Implementing Entrepreneurial Operating System (EOS)?** PAS strengthens your Accountability Chart by clarifying who keeps which promises.
- **Following Scaling Up or similar methodologies?** PAS becomes the alignment layer that connects your Core Values to daily operations.
- **Tracking Net Promoter Score (NPS), Customer Satisfaction Score (CSAT), or other customer health scores?** PAS shows you *why* those scores move and gives you a system to improve them.
- **Managing remote or offshore teams?** PAS gives distributed teams the shared truth they need to work aligned.

PAS isn't a replacement. It's the connective tissue that makes everything else work better.

If you're already measuring what matters - team engagement, customer satisfaction, operational efficiency - then PAS gives you the system to actually move those metrics in the right direction.

Why This Matters for Your Team, Your Customers, and Your Metrics.

You already know what matters:

Your teams shouldn't feel set up to fail. They shouldn't be apologizing for promises they didn't make or scrambling to deliver outcomes they can't control.

Your customers shouldn't feel confused, misled, or surprised. They should know exactly what they're getting and get exactly what was promised.

Your metrics should improve because the system works, not because you're gaming the numbers or burning out your people.

If you care about these things, you're already doing the hard work. You're tracking NPS. You're running employee engagement surveys. You're measuring delivery timelines, support response rates, customer retention, and operational efficiency.

PAS doesn't replace those efforts. It makes them easier.

Because when promises are aligned:

- Teams feel confident instead of stressed (your engagement scores improve)
- Customers feel clear instead of confused (your NPS and retention climb)
- Systems work reliably instead of chaotically (your operational metrics stabilize)
- Leaders make decisions from shared truth instead of conflicting data (your meetings get shorter and more productive)

You're already measuring what matters. PAS gives you the system to actually improve it.

Why Promises Matter Now More Than Ever

The world has changed.

Customers expect instant clarity.

Teams are distributed.

Workflows are automated.

AI agents speak on behalf of brands.

Documentation lives everywhere.

Expectations form in seconds.

Patience is thin.

Companies no longer compete on product alone. They compete on **predictability.** On **trust.** On how reliably they keep their word.

A good product will win you customers.

A clear promise will keep them.

A kept promise will grow them.

This book is not about perfection. **It's about alignment.**

It's about building a culture, an identity, and an operating process that ensures your company promises only what it can deliver—and delivers exactly what it promises. Every time.

If Your Company Has Ever Said 'Yes' When It Should Have Said 'Not Yet'... This Book Is For You.

If your customers ever felt confused, misled, or surprised—this book will show you why.

If your teams ever felt stressed, stretched, or unsure—this book will give them clarity.

If your leaders ever felt pulled in too many directions—this book will give them one truth.

If your systems, AI, or automations ever made promises without your approval—this book will give you control.

And if you've ever wanted to build a company that grows with trust instead of chaos, alignment instead of drift, and clarity instead of confusion—this book will show you the path.

PART ONE
THE AXISLINE FABLE

ONE
THE YEAR OF
GOOD INTENTIONS

Marcus Patel, CEO of AxisLine, noticed the silence first.

Not the comfortable kind, the kind that settles over a team deep in flow. This was the other kind. The held-breath kind. The *something's-wrong-but-no-one-wants-to-say-it* kind.

He stood outside the conference room, one hand on the door handle, watching his leadership team through the glass. They were already seated for the weekly check-in, but no one was talking. Rina Chen, the CMO, typed furiously on her laptop, jaw tight. Theo Park, CRO, scrolled his phone with the aggressive thumb-swipes of someone avoiding eye contact. Tessa Ruiz, Head of Delivery, stared at a spot on the table like she was solving an equation in her head.

Devon Carter, Head of Support, wasn't there yet. Late again.

Marcus pushed through the door.

"Morning," he said, trying to sound lighter than he felt.

"Morning," came the scattered replies. Polite. Automatic. Empty.

He sat down and opened his laptop. The quarterly dashboard loaded—a riot of green metrics and upward-trending arrows. Revenue up 43%. New customers up 51%. Marketing engagement through the roof.

Everything looks great, he thought. *So why does it feel like we're falling apart?*

Rina spoke first, launching into her update with the rehearsed energy of someone who'd practiced it.

"Big week! Our new campaign is generating insane traffic. We're trending on Product Hunt. Prospects are loving the messaging—especially the AI work-flow stuff."

She clicked through slides showing website analytics, ad performance, click-through rates. All impressive. All climbing.

But Marcus watched the room, not the screen.

Devon—who'd just slipped in late—gave a thin smile that didn't reach his eyes.

Tessa's pen hovered over her notebook but didn't move.

Theo leaned back in his chair, arms crossed, nodding along but looking... bored? Defensive? It was hard to tell.

"Sales is pacing ahead of target," Theo said when Rina finished. He said it like a challenge. "We're on track to hit the highest quarterly bookings in company history."

Another flicker of discomfort rippled across the table.

Marcus saw it. He always saw it.

"Tess?" he asked. "How's Delivery?"

Tessa closed her notebook. Slowly. Deliberately.

"Busy," she said.

That single word landed like a stone.

Marcus leaned forward. "Busy how?"

She met his eyes. Held them. Then looked away.

"Busy," she repeated.

The meeting ended the way it always did—scattered, vague commitments to "circle back" and "sync up later." Everyone rushed out to their next call.

Except Tessa.

She stayed in her seat, staring at her phone. Marcus lingered too, pretending to close his laptop while he waited.

Finally, she spoke.

"We need to talk."

Marcus sat back down. "About the 'busy'?"

"About the broken."

That word hung in the air between them.

"What's going on?" he asked quietly.

Tessa rubbed her temples. She looked exhausted. Not the good kind of exhausted that comes from hard work. The kind that comes from fighting a losing battle.

"Customer expectations are..." She paused, searching for the right word. "Everywhere. Every deal coming in has different assumptions. Some think we offer features we don't. Others expect timelines that aren't remotely possible. My team is improvising. Every. Single. Day."

"Improvising how?"

"We're cleaning up promises we didn't make."

Marcus felt something cold settle in his chest.

Tessa kept going, her voice dropping to almost a whisper. "And we're getting escalation messages from the offshore team at 3 AM. They're panicking because the AI chatbot is telling customers things that don't exist."

"Like what?"

"A 'predictive scheduling engine.'"

Marcus blinked. "We don't have predictive scheduling."

"I know," Tessa said. "But *someone*—or *something*—is telling customers we do. And when they can't find it, they escalate. And then my team scrambles. And then we all look incompetent."

Marcus stared past her, his mind racing.

The growth. The new messaging. The AI enhancements. The pressure on sales. The stressed delivery team. The late nights. The vague answers in meetings.

It wasn't random. It was a pattern.

"Marcus," Tessa said softly, "this isn't a small problem anymore."

He met her eyes. And in that moment, he realized something that made his stomach drop:

The year of good intentions was leading them somewhere they'd never intended to go.

"Okay," he said. "Let's dig in."

But he had no idea how deep the problem really went.

Or how much everything was about to change.

TWO
THE SURPRISING NUMBERS

Marcus liked numbers because numbers didn't lie.

These numbers, though? They made him want to throw his laptop across the room.

He sat alone in his office at 6:47 AM on a gray Tuesday, staring at the quarterly customer health dashboard. The early morning light barely penetrated the fog outside, and the office was silent except for the hum of the HVAC and the occasional ping of Slack notifications he was ignoring.

The dashboard looked fine at first glance. Colorful. Organized. Professional.

Then he read the actual numbers:

Renewals: Down 11%

Customer complaints: Up 23%

Support resolution time: Up 38%

Average onboarding duration: 39 days (was 21)

NPS: 27 (was 56)

He sat back. Rubbed his eyes. Read them again.

Still bad.

"This doesn't make sense," he muttered to the empty room.

AxisLine just had its *best sales quarter in company history*. Marketing campaigns were landing. The AI-powered workflow engine was getting buzz. They'd hired twelve new people in the last two months alone.

Everything should be getting *better*.

Instead, it was quietly falling apart.

He clicked into the customer feedback log. The comments came fast:

"The platform looked easier in the demo than in real life."

"Support told me something different than Sales did."

"I got three different answers from three different people. Which one is true?"

"Your AI chatbot keeps promising features that don't exist."

"I'm confused. What exactly does this platform DO?"

Marcus scrolled. More of the same. Page after page.

Then he saw it, a red flag from the support dashboard:

ALERT: Rising Cross-Team Conflicts

Pattern Detected: Misaligned Expectations

Support tools didn't usually editorialize. They reported. They tracked. They didn't *diagnose*.

If the system itself was calling out conflicts, things were worse than he thought.

A soft knock interrupted his spiral.

Rina stood in the doorway, clutching a coffee mug with both hands. Her expression mirrored his.

"You seeing this too?" she asked.

Marcus turned his screen toward her.

She closed her eyes. Took a breath. "I was afraid of that."

She sat down across from him. Didn't ask permission. Just sat.

"We're driving so much interest," she said quietly. "So many prospects. So much demand. But after they sign..." She trailed off.

"They're disappointed," Marcus finished.

"That's the polite version."

Rina set her mug down and leaned forward, elbows on her knees, hands pressed together like she was praying.

"My team's been fighting fires all week. Sales says Product isn't delivering what they promised. Product says Marketing set the wrong expectations. Sales says Support is too slow. Support says they're drowning in unclear tickets. And our offshore team—" She laughed bitterly. "—they're pinging me at 3 AM asking for clarification because *they don't know what's real anymore.*"

Marcus felt the weight of it settling on his shoulders.

"And the AI?" he asked carefully.

Rina's jaw tightened. "The chatbot is... creative. It's telling customers we have predictive scheduling. And hyper-flex automations. And customizable dashboards."

"We don't have any of those."

"I know," she said. "But the bot learned those phrases from our old landing pages. From high-performing ad copy. From webinar transcripts we forgot existed." She paused. "We trained it on our own hype."

The silence stretched between them.

Finally, Marcus said what they were both thinking: "Something is fundamentally off. The more we grow, the worse this gets."

Rina nodded slowly. "It's like the company is being stretched from the inside."

She leaned back, studied him. "Have you talked to Tessa?"

"Yesterday."

"Then you know Delivery is barely keeping up. Her team is improvising. Every. Single. Day."

Marcus pulled up Tessa's calendar. Forty-two meetings in the next three days. That wasn't a schedule. That was someone drowning.

Rina stood up. "We can't market our way out of this. We can't sell our way out of it. We can't charm our way out of it."

"No," Marcus said softly. "Not this time."

He took a breath. Made a decision.

"We need to call a leadership meeting. Today. Before this spirals into something we can't undo."

Rina nodded. "I'll gather the team."

She paused in the doorway. "Marcus... whatever's happening, it's not a small fix."

He looked at the dashboard again. All those red numbers. All those frustrated customers. All that drift.

"No," he said. "It's not."

AxisLine wasn't just growing.

It was drifting.

And the numbers were finally telling the truth.

THREE
ESCALATIONS EVERYWHERE

The conference room felt smaller than usual.

Maybe it was the tension. Maybe it was the way everyone sat a little farther apart than normal, like they were afraid of catching something contagious.

Tessa Ruiz, Head of Delivery, arrived first, dropped into a chair, and immediately started scrolling her phone. The unread message counter said **119**. She didn't even try to hide it.

Devon Carter, Head of Support, came next, rubbing his temples with both hands. "I haven't seen escalation volume like this," he muttered to no one in particular. "Not even during the outage."

Rina Chen, CMO, and Theo Park, CRO, arrived together but didn't make eye contact. They sat on opposite sides of the table.

Marcus stood at the front of the room, watching them settle. Or try to settle. No one looked settled.

"Thanks for coming on short notice," he said. "We have a situation."

Devon let out a short, humorless laugh. "*That's* an understatement."

"Let's start with Support," Marcus said. "Devon, walk us through it."

Devon tapped his laptop. A dashboard appeared on the screen.

It was a wall of red.

- **148 open escalations**
- **72-hour median response time** (SLA is 24)
- **Customer escalation severity: Trending up**
- **AI misrouting tickets: 34% of total volume**
- **Offshore team requesting clarification: 40% of tickets**

"Forty percent?" Rina whispered.

Devon nodded grimly. "They don't know how to answer questions because customers are asking about things we don't actually *do*."

He pulled up a sample of recent tickets:

"Where's the predictive scheduler I was promised?"

"Sales told me there's hyper-flex automation. Where is it?"

"Support says this is impossible, but Sales told me it's easy. Who's lying?"

"Your AI agent said there's a clean-up wizard for bad data. I can't find it."

"Why does onboarding say something completely different from Sales?"

The room went quiet.

"Who told them these things?" Marcus asked.

Devon raised his eyebrows. "Take your pick. Sales scripts. Old marketing copy. Webinar transcripts from 2023. Third-party review sites that scraped our old site. And..." He hesitated. "Our AI chatbot."

"*What* did the chatbot do?" Tessa asked, her voice sharp.

Devon clicked a tab labeled **AI Response Audit**.

"It learned from a mix of old documentation, unvetted case studies, and outdated product manuals. It's pulling from all of it and stitching together features that..." He paused. "...technically never existed."

"Like what?" Tessa demanded.

Devon turned the screen toward her.

"Like a 'one-click integration wizard for custom workflows.'"

Tessa's face went white. "We've *never* had that. That would take six engineers six months to build."

"The AI doesn't know that," Devon said quietly.

Marcus turned to Tessa. "What about Delivery?"

Tessa exhaled sharply. Set her phone face-down on the table. When she spoke, her voice was tight with exhaustion.

"Onboarding timelines are slipping. Badly. Customers show up expecting the platform to do things we didn't design it to do. That leads to custom requests. Custom requests slow us down. That delays everyone else. It's a cascade."

"How many customers are asking for custom workflows?" Marcus asked.

Tessa didn't answer right away.

Devon looked over. "Tessa. How many?"

She swallowed. "Eighty percent."

"*Eighty percent?*" Rina said, her voice rising. "That can't be right."

"It's right," Tessa snapped. "And they all *swear* that someone—Sales, Marketing, Support, the damn chatbot told them it was included. So now *my* team looks like liars when we say it's not."

She lifted her phone. "And our offshore onboarding team is drowning because they're following documentation that hasn't been updated in *eighteen months*."

Marcus felt his stomach drop. "We've updated the product three times since then."

"I *know*," Tessa said. "That's the problem."

Rina spoke next, her voice quieter than usual. Almost defeated.

"Marketing is getting hammered online. People are posting screenshots of chatbot promises and comparing them to what we actually deliver."

She pulled up a tweet on her laptop:

"Love AxisLine's concept. Hate that half the features they advertise are imaginary."

Another:

"Support is great. But why is your AI agent lying to me?"

And a brutal one:

"Nothing matches what their website says. NOTHING."

Rina closed her laptop with a soft click. "This is turning into a credibility problem. Fast."

Marcus sat down.

The room was silent except for the faint buzz of the projector and someone's foot tapping nervously against the chair leg.

"Let's stop for a second," Marcus said. "We're all seeing the symptoms. But what's actually *causing* this? What's the root?"

No one spoke.

The quiet stretched.

Finally, Devon said it: "We're making promises we can't keep."

Tessa added: "Or promises we didn't mean to make."

Rina added: "Or promises we didn't even *know* we were making."

Marcus nodded slowly.

"We're drifting," he said. "And the bigger we get, the faster we drift."

The truth of it settled over the room like smoke.

FOUR
THE MEETING NO ONE WANTED

By 2:00 PM, they were back in the same glass-walled conference room.

But this time, no one looked optimistic.

The room felt tight. Humid with anxiety. The whiteboard still had half-erased sketches from last week's product roadmap session—a reminder of a time when they thought they had time.

Marcus stood at the head of the table. No slides. No charts. No sugar-coating.

"Thank you for coming," he said. "We have a problem. A serious one."

That got everyone's attention.

Theo leaned back in his chair, arms crossed. His default posture when he was about to dig in.

"Before we call this a *crisis*," he said, "let's be clear about what we're even talking about. Sales is crushing targets. We're not the ones struggling here."

Devon's jaw tightened. "*Your deals* are the reason Support is underwater."

"Oh, here we go—"

"*Enough*," Marcus said sharply.

The room went silent.

"This isn't about Sales or Support or Delivery or Product or Marketing," Marcus continued. "It's about *all of us*. We're growing fast, but the experience we're delivering is coming apart at the seams."

He turned on the projector.

A single slide appeared:

What We Promise vs. What We Deliver

That alone was enough to make the room uncomfortable.

Rina shifted in her seat. "Look, some messaging may have drifted a bit during scaling. That happens. We can tighten it up."

"It's not just messaging," Marcus said.

He clicked once.

A list of recent customer complaints appeared:

- *"I was told integration takes one day. It took two weeks."*
- *"Your bot said I'd get predictive scheduling. Where is it?"*
- *"Sales said onboarding was included. Delivery says it's extra."*
- *"Three teams, three different answers."*
- *"I don't know what AxisLine actually does anymore."*

Theo leaned forward, his voice sharp. "These are cherry-picked."

"*Still not listening*," Devon snapped. "These aren't cherry-picked. This is the *pattern*."

Tessa opened her notebook. "My team logged ninety-seven customer requests last month for features we've never offered. Ninety. Seven."

"That's not possible," Theo said.

Tessa met his eyes. "It's happening."

"And offshore support is asking for clarification on *forty percent* of tickets," Devon added. "Forty. That's not a rounding error, Theo. They're confused. Customers are confused. And all of it traces back to promises, explicit and implicit, that don't align."

The room went still.

Marcus took a slow breath.

"We are unintentionally making promises everywhere. Humans. Systems. Bots. Documentation. Outdated assets. Ad copy from last year. Even old webinar transcripts are being indexed by our AI and used as 'truth.'"

Everyone stared at him.

  THE MEETING NO ONE WANTED

"It's like every part of the company is speaking its own dialect of our brand," he said.

Rina frowned. "And customers are hearing all of them at once."

Tessa nodded. "And *my* team is expected to make all those dialects match reality."

"I didn't authorize any of this," Theo muttered.

"*No one* authorized it," Marcus said. "That's the point. It's happening anyway. We're drifting."

The silence that followed was heavy.

Then Rina asked the question everyone was thinking: "So what do we do about it?"

Marcus looked down at his hands. There was a weight to his silence.

"I know someone who can help," he finally said. "Someone I've worked with before."

Theo groaned. "Another consultant? We don't need another slide deck about 'improving cross-functional communication.'"

Marcus shook his head. "He's not like that. He doesn't start with communication. He doesn't even start with strategy."

"Then what does he start with?" Tessa asked.

"Promises," Marcus said. "He helps companies understand the promises they make, internally and externally, and why they fail to keep them."

Devon raised an eyebrow. "And this... works?"

Marcus met his eyes. "It saved my last company. We were six weeks from imploding when I brought him in. Three months later, we'd turned it around completely."

"Why didn't you mention this before?" Rina asked.

"Because," Marcus said quietly, "I didn't think we needed it yet."

He paused.

"I was wrong."

Theo crossed his arms. "So what, we're supposed to sit in a room and talk about 'promises'? Sounds like corporate therapy."

"Maybe that's exactly what we need," Devon said.

Theo shot him a look.

Marcus stepped in. "Look, I'm not asking you to like it. I'm asking you to trust me. Just for one session. If it's a waste of time, we'll kill it and move on."

The room was quiet.

Finally, Tessa spoke. "When can he start?"

"Tomorrow," Marcus said. "If we say yes."

Another silence.

Then, one by one, they nodded.

Even Theo.

"Fine," he said. "But if this guy shows up with a whiteboard and a bunch of trust-fall exercises, I'm out."

Marcus almost smiled. "Deal."

FIVE
ENTER VICTOR LANE

Victor Lane stood in the lobby of AxisLine's office, observing.

He didn't take notes. Didn't pull out his phone. Just stood there, hands in his pockets, watching.

The receptionist was on a call, her voice strained: *"I understand, but let me connect you with someone who can explain what we actually offer..."*

A support rep hurried past, whispering into her headset: *"I know Sales said that, but let me explain what we can actually do..."*

A customer success manager paced near the windows, frustration leaking into her voice: *"That's not how the platform works. I'm not sure who told you that..."*

A product manager rushed past a group of engineers, muttering something about Marketing "over-promising again."

Victor filed each observation away.

He didn't judge.

He didn't diagnose.

He simply noticed.

And what he noticed was drift. The kind you could feel in the air.

The receptionist looked up. "You must be Victor?"

He smiled warmly. "That's me."

"I'll let Marcus know you're here."

"No rush," Victor said. "I'm learning already."

Upstairs, the leadership team gathered in the conference room. Nervous energy hummed like a fluorescent light about to flicker out.

Marcus paced. Rina straightened her laptop for the tenth time. Theo scrolled through Slack, pretending to be unbothered.

Devon and Tessa whispered by the wall:

"Does he do culture work?"

"Is he a systems person?"

"Leadership coach maybe?"

"Please don't let this be a trust-fall exercise."

Marcus checked his watch. "He should be here any—"

The door opened.

Victor entered with the kind of quiet confidence that made the room go still. Not intimidating. Not performative. Just... present.

He wore a simple navy blazer, no laptop, no binder, no bag. He greeted each person with a direct handshake and steady eye contact.

"Thank you for having me," he said, taking a seat at the table.

Theo leaned back, arms already crossed. "So what exactly do you *do*, Victor?"

Victor looked at him. Not long. Not challenging. Just long enough to signal he'd heard the question fully.

"I help companies understand the promises they make," he said, "and why they fail to keep them."

Rina tilted her head. "Promises?"

"Promises," Victor repeated. "Every company makes them. Most don't realize how many."

He sat forward.

"But every promise your company makes is either strengthening your business... or slowly breaking it."

Theo smirked. "Okay, but we didn't call you in over a *slogan*. We're dealing with real issues: sales, support, onboarding, AI errors, offshore confusion, angry customers"

Victor held up his hand gently. Not dismissive. Just... clear.

"And I'm telling you," he said calmly, "those aren't issues. Those are *symptoms*."

The room tensed.

"What's the issue, then?" Devon asked.

Victor looked around the table, meeting each pair of eyes.

"You've lost alignment," he said softly.

Silence.

"You're making promises you can't keep. Not intentionally. Never intentionally. But drift doesn't require intent. It only requires growth without clarity."

Marcus exhaled slowly. He'd known this. But hearing it out loud hit differently.

"Before I tell you anything," Victor continued, "I need to ask *you* a question."

He let the quiet stretch just long enough to make them lean in.

"What is your company's Core Promise?"

Marcus opened his mouth, but Tessa spoke first.

"We deliver automated workflows for operational teams."

Victor shook his head gently. "That's what you *sell*. Not what you *promise*."

Rina tried. "We help companies streamline their processes."

"That," Victor said, "is an aspiration. Not a promise."

Theo jumped in. "We make operations more efficient."

"That," Victor replied, "is an outcome. Not a promise."

He turned to Devon.

"Support?"

Devon hesitated. "We promise to be responsive?"

Victor smiled gently. "No. That's your *hope*. Not your promise."

He leaned back in his chair.

"You see the problem."

No one spoke.

Victor's tone stayed steady, but there was warmth in it. Not judgment.

"If you can't articulate your Core Promise internally, then your teams—human or AI—will make up their own.

Your offshore support teams will guess.

Your marketing will inflate.

Your sales team will improvise.

Your product will interpret.

Your AI will hallucinate.

And your customers will confuse possibility with reality."

A chill ran through the room.

Even Theo stopped shifting in his chair.

Victor folded his hands.

"This isn't a problem with your *people*," he said. "It's a problem with your *promises*. And until we fix that, everything else will continue to drift."

He stood up.

"So let's begin."

The transformation of AxisLine had officially started.

SIX

PROMISE MAKERS &
PROMISE KEEPERS

Victor walked to the whiteboard and uncapped a marker.

He didn't draw a pyramid.

He didn't sketch a funnel.

He didn't diagram a system.

He wrote just four words:

Promise Makers

Promise Keepers

Then he turned back to the team.

"These," he said, tapping the board, "are the two forces inside every company."

The group looked confused.

"We're not talking about departments?" Rina asked.

"No," Victor replied. "Departments are *costumes*. Roles are costumes. Titles are costumes. But *this*" he pointed again "is who you really are."

Theo crossed his arms. "Okay, so which one is Sales?"

Victor smiled. "You tell me."

Theo smirked. "Promise Makers, obviously."

"Correct," Victor said. "Sales makes promises to help customers buy. Marketing makes promises to help them understand. Product makes promises to help them imagine possibilities."

He circled **Promise Makers**.

"These teams shape expectations."

Then he motioned to the other side of the board.

"And *these* teams" he tapped **Promise Keepers** "fulfill those expectations. Delivery. Support. Onboarding. Implementation. Engineering. Operations. Your offshore teams. Your automations. Even your AI agents."

"AI?" Devon repeated.

Victor nodded. "If it interacts with a customer, it's making a promise. If it performs work, it's keeping a promise. AI and automation do both."

That landed hard.

Rina leaned forward slowly. "So you're saying our problems aren't because of any one department."

"I'm saying," Victor replied, "your Promise Makers and your Promise Keepers are living in different realities."

He let that sink in.

Tessa spoke next. "But we're all working toward the same goals."

Victor tilted his head. "*Are* you?"

He pointed to Rina. "Marketing wants reach and resonance."

Then to Theo. "Sales wants revenue."

Then to Tessa. "Delivery wants repeatability."

Then to Devon. "Support wants stability."

Then to the empty chair where Product sat. "Engineering wants feasibility."

"And the offshore teams," Victor added gently, "want *clarity*."

It was true. Uncomfortably true.

"Look," Victor said, pacing slowly, "no one here is *wrong*. But you're not *aligned*. And when Promise Makers and Promise Keepers drift apart, the customer becomes the rope in a very painful game of tug-of-war."

                    PROMISE MAKERS & PROMISE KEEPERS

Tessa rubbed her face with both hands. "Yep. That sounds about right."

Victor paced in front of the whiteboard.

"Promise Makers dream big. They open doors. They tell the world who you are."

He tapped the other side.

"Promise Keepers carry the weight of those dreams... and deliver the reality."

He capped the marker.

"Both are essential. But they have to speak the same language."

Theo leaned forward. "So what's *causing* the misalignment?"

Victor gave him a long, almost sympathetic look.

"Growth."

He let the word hang in the air like smoke.

"When you were small, everyone naturally shared the same understanding. The same truths. The same promises. You didn't *need* a system to stay aligned."

He placed the marker on the table.

"But as you grew—new people, new systems, new automations, new AI layers, new offshore teams—you *assumed* that alignment would scale automatically."

He shook his head softly.

"It never does."

He turned back to the board.

"Promise Makers kept evolving the story.

Promise Keepers kept evolving the delivery.

But no one was making sure they stayed connected."

He drew a line between the two columns. Then erased part of it.

"And when that connection breaks..." He gestured at the gap. "Drift."

The room was silent.

Marcus finally spoke. "So how do we fix it?"

Victor turned to him.

"That," he said, "is exactly what we're about to figure out."

SEVEN

THE HIDDEN COST OF DRIFT

AxisLine always looked good from the outside.

Modern lobby. Sleek branding. Fast-paced energy. Awards on the wall. Fresh capital in the bank. Talented people hustling through the halls.

But Victor Lane knew better than to trust surfaces.

After the leadership meeting adjourned, he asked Marcus if he could walk the floor alone. Marcus hesitated, just for a second, then nodded.

Victor moved through the office like a doctor making rounds. Quietly. Observing. Not diagnosing yet. Just noticing.

He stopped first at the Delivery pod.

A young onboarding specialist named Jasmine sat hunched over her keyboard, nine tabs open, shoulders up near her ears. Her desktop was chaos: half-written emails, mismatched documentation, Slack threads blinking red.

"Hi there," Victor said gently.

She jumped. "Oh! Sorry, I didn't see you." Forced smile. "Can I help you with something?"

"Just walking around. Busy day?"

She laughed, the kind without humor. "Every day is busy."

Victor glanced at her screen. "What are you working on?"

Jasmine exhaled slowly, like she'd been holding her breath for hours.

"Trying to reconcile what our biggest new customer says they were promised in their demo, which is apparently what drove their decision to buy, versus what we actually offer. Because that feature? We sunset it last quarter."

She rubbed her eyes. "This happens more and more. The expectations don't match the platform."

"And how does that feel?" Victor asked.

She considered the question. Really considered it.

"Honestly? Exhausting. I feel like the bad guy. Customers come in excited, and I have to be the one who tells them what we *can't* do." She paused. "Sometimes I wonder if the people selling this have ever actually *used* it."

Victor didn't respond. Didn't need to.

He just nodded. Made a note. Moved on.

<hr>

Next stop: Support.

Two agents worked through a queue that never seemed to shrink. Their screens showed 47 open tickets. 52. 59. The number kept climbing even as they typed.

"Tell them I'm escalating this to Engineering," one whispered urgently.

"But Engineering said they're not touching custom workflows anymore," the other whispered back.

"Doesn't matter. Customer was promised it."

"*By who?*"

Long pause.

"Good question."

Victor stood there for a moment. Neither agent had noticed him. They were too deep in the firefight.

He pulled up the offshore support team's Slack channel on a large monitor near the break room.

Messages streamed in fast:

Can someone clarify this feature? Customer swears it exists.

The customer says onboarding told them X but documentation says Y. Which is correct?

Which version of the workflow editor should I reference? I'm seeing three different ones.

AI bot is referencing something I can't find in training materials. Help?

Need guidance ASAP. Customer is angry.

The timestamps made Victor's chest tighten:

1:47 AM

2:13 AM

3:06 AM

4:22 AM

The invisible cost of drift was sleepless nights in another time zone. People halfway around the world, panicking in the dark, trying to figure out what was real.

He walked further until he reached a corner where two product managers were arguing in harsh whispers.

"We can't just build features because Sales keeps promising them," one said, voice tight with frustration.

"Well maybe if we built *something* like it, they'd stop making shit up," the other shot back.

Victor paused. Listened.

Neither person was wrong. Neither was right. They were both just tired of being blamed for something they didn't cause.

Finally, he made his way back to the front lobby.

A custodian was wiping down the large AxisLine mission statement etched into the wall:

Empowering teams with intelligent workflows.

Victor read it twice.

Aspirational. Vague. Open to interpretation.

Too open.

A phrase that allowed a hundred different promises, none of them aligned.

He pulled out his phone and took a picture. He'd come back to this later.

When Victor returned to the conference room, Marcus was waiting, arms crossed, staring out the window.

"Well?" Marcus asked without turning around. "How bad is it?"

Victor set his notebook on the table.

"Marcus," he said softly, "your people don't know what you stand for. Not because they're confused... but because the company itself hasn't decided."

Marcus turned. His jaw was tight. "We're growing. Things are messy when you grow. That's normal."

"Growth is messy," Victor agreed. "Drift is deadly."

He flipped open his notebook.

"Here's what I saw."

He read from his notes, his voice quiet but firm:

- "Your delivery team is apologizing for promises they didn't make."
- "Your support team is compensating for systems that promise the wrong things."
- "Your offshore team is working in the dark at 3 AM because documentation isn't aligned."
- "Your AI agent is recycling legacy promises no one remembers making."
- "Your product team is being pressured to build ghost features."
- "Your sales team is improvising to win deals."
- "Your marketing team is amplifying a story that isn't anchored in reality."

He closed the notebook.

"And all of it is creating a culture where your people feel like they're failing... even when they're not."

Marcus sat down heavily. The weight of it settled on his shoulders like a wet coat.

"This isn't a people problem," Victor said gently. "It's a promise problem."

Marcus looked up. "So where do we start?"

Victor smiled. Not the confident consultant smile. Something softer. More human.

"With the one promise that matters most."

He tapped his notebook.

"Tomorrow, we define your Core Promise. And once we do... everything else will begin to make sense."

As Marcus gathered his things, he took one last look around the office through the glass walls.

For the first time, he saw it clearly.

The exhaustion.

The confusion.

The frustration.

The quiet chaos.

They weren't failing because they were bad at their jobs.

They were failing because the company had drifted so far from its promises that no one knew what truth they were supposed to keep.

But tomorrow, they would begin the journey back.

And it would start with one question:

Who are we, really, when we make a promise?

EIGHT
THE CORE PROMISE

The next morning, the leadership team filed into the conference room with a strange mix of anticipation and dread.

Today wasn't about diagnosing the problem.

Today was about truth.

Victor was already there, standing by the whiteboard with a cup of black coffee, looking... tired? Marcus noticed it for the first time. Victor's confidence was still there, but there was something else underneath it. Doubt? Uncertainty?

"Morning," Victor said. His voice was warm, but it didn't have quite the same ease as yesterday.

No one replied with quite the same ease either.

Theo settled in with his arms crossed. Default posture.

Rina sat forward, notebook open, pen ready.

Devon slumped into his chair like he'd already run a marathon.

Tessa looked alert but wary.

Marcus took his usual seat at the head of the table.

Victor uncapped his marker. Stared at the blank whiteboard for a moment. Then wrote:

THE CORE PROMISE: THE PROMISE YOU MUST KEEP — EVERY TIME.

"The Core Promise," Victor said, turning to face them, "is the single outcome your company guarantees to deliver, no matter what. It's not what you *hope* to provide. Not what you *want* to provide. Not what your marketing *says* you provide."

He paused.

"It's what you *actually* provide: consistently, reliably, predictably. Every single time."

Theo shifted. "Okay, but we already have a mission statement. 'Empowering teams with intelligent workflows.' That's our thing."

Victor wrote it on the board.

Then he turned back to Theo. "Is that what you promise?"

"That's what we *do*," Theo said.

"No," Victor replied gently. "That's what you *hope* happens when people use your product. But what do you *guarantee*?"

Silence.

Victor grabbed a chair, flipped it around, and sat facing them. For the first time, he didn't look like a consultant. He looked like someone trying to solve a puzzle he wasn't sure had a solution.

"Yesterday," he said, "I asked you what your Core Promise was. Do you remember what you said?"

A few uncomfortable nods.

Victor stood up and wrote their answers on the board from memory:

"We deliver automated workflows for operational teams." — Tessa

"We help companies streamline their processes." — Rina

"We make operations more efficient." — Theo

"We promise to be responsive." — Devon

He stepped back and studied the list.

"These weren't wrong," he said. "But they weren't *promises* either."

He pointed to Tessa's answer. "This is what you *sell*."

He pointed to Rina's. "This is an *aspiration*."

He pointed to Theo's. "This is an *outcome*."

He pointed to Devon's. "This is a *hope*."

Theo leaned forward, irritation creeping into his voice. "Okay, so what's the difference? We sell automation. It makes them efficient. That's the promise."

Victor turned to him. His expression softened.

"The difference," he said slowly, "is that a promise is something you *control*. An outcome is something the customer experiences *if everything goes right*."

He walked back to the board.

"You can't promise efficiency, Theo. You can't control whether they use your product well. You can't guarantee they'll set it up right or train their team or integrate it properly."

He turned back to face them.

"So the question isn't what you *hope* to deliver. It's what you can *guarantee* to deliver. Every time. Without fail."

Theo's jaw tightened. "So what *can* we guarantee?"

Victor stopped. Stared at the whiteboard.

Then he did something unexpected.

He sat down.

"I don't know yet," he admitted.

The room went still.

Rina blinked. "You... don't know?"

Victor turned to her. And for the first time, he looked uncertain.

"Not yet," he said. "Because I'm not the one who has to keep it. *You* are."

He leaned forward, elbows on his knees.

"Yesterday, you gave me four different answers because you're thinking about what you *want* to promise. What you *sell*. What you *hope* happens."

He looked around the table.

"Today, we need to find what you can *actually* promise. And that's harder. Because it has to pass three tests."

He stood and wrote them on the board:

1. Can you deliver it EVERY TIME?

2. Can you deliver it WITHOUT HEROICS?

3. Can your ENTIRE TEAM, human and AI, deliver it consistently?

"If the answer to any of those is no," Victor said, "it's not your Core Promise. It's still an aspiration."

He capped the marker. Turned back to them.

"So let's stop thinking about what you sell. Let's start thinking about what every customer, every single one, actually gets when they work with you."

Tessa spoke next. Her voice was quiet but firm.

"We can promise clarity."

Everyone turned to look at her.

"Think about it," she said. "Every complaint we get, every escalation, every confused customer—it all comes down to clarity. They don't know what we do. They don't know what's included. They don't know what to expect."

She looked around the table.

"What if our promise is just... making it clear? Making workflows simple to understand. Making expectations clear. Making the platform clear."

Victor wrote it on the board:

"We make workflows clear."

Stared at it.

"Can you deliver that every time?" he asked.

Tessa thought about it. "If we fix our documentation. If we align our messag-

                                    THE CORE PROMISE

ing. If we train offshore properly. If we constrain the AI..." She paused. "Yeah. I think we can."

"Without heroics?" Victor asked.

She nodded slowly. "It's work. But it's not impossible."

"Can your entire team deliver it?" Victor asked.

Devon jumped in. "If we have a clear promise to point to, yeah. Support can deliver clarity. We'd finally have something to anchor to."

Rina was nodding. "Marketing can work with that. It's specific. It's defensible. It's not hype."

Theo was quiet. Arms still crossed.

"Theo?" Marcus asked.

Theo exhaled. "I don't love it. But..." He looked at the board. "I also can't argue with it. Sales *can* promise clarity. We can show them exactly what they're getting. No surprises."

He shrugged. "Yeah. Okay. I'm in."

Victor stepped back from the board.

"We simplify complex workflows so they're immediately clear."

He wrote it clean:

CORE PROMISE: "We simplify complex workflows so they're immediately clear."

Then he turned to them.

"This is it. This is what you keep. Every time. No exceptions. No heroics. Just this."

The room was quiet.

Marcus stared at the board. It felt... small. Simple. Almost too simple.

"Is it enough?" he asked.

Victor smiled. And this time, the confidence was back.

"It's everything," he said. "Because it's real."

But the work wasn't done.

Next, they'd have to build the Stack.

And that's when things would get harder.

THE PROMISE STACK

The energy in the room was different now.

They had a Core Promise. Something solid. Something real.

But Victor wasn't celebrating yet.

"Now comes the hard part," he said, erasing the board.

Theo groaned. "*That* was the easy part?"

"That," Victor said, "was clarity. This is accountability."

He drew five horizontal lines across the whiteboard, stacked like layers.

1. CORE PROMISE

2. SUPPORTING PROMISES

3. CONDITIONAL PROMISES

4. EXPERIMENTAL PROMISES

5. LEGACY PROMISES

"This," Victor said, "is your Promise Stack. Every promise your company makes fits into one of these five layers."

He pointed at the top.

"Core Promise—you already have it. One promise. The anchor."

Then he moved down.

"Supporting Promises—these are the operational promises that MUST work for your Core Promise to be kept. If a Supporting Promise breaks, your Core Promise breaks."

Rina leaned forward. "Like what?"

"Like documentation that's accurate," Victor said. "Like onboarding that matches what Sales promised. Like your AI agent giving answers that align with reality."

He moved to the third layer.

"Conditional Promises, these are real promises, but only under specific conditions. 'We can integrate with your system... *if* it uses standard APIs.' 'We can customize workflows... *if* you're on the Enterprise plan.'"

Tessa nodded. "So we stop saying 'yes' when we mean 'maybe.'"

"Exactly," Victor said.

He pointed to the fourth layer.

"Experimental Promises, these are things you're testing. Beta features. Prototypes. Ideas. They're NOT promises yet. They stay internal until they pass quality gates."

Then the bottom layer.

"Legacy Promises, promises that used to be true but aren't anymore. Old features. Sunset capabilities. Outdated messaging. These need to be KILLED. Publicly. Clearly. Or they keep haunting you."

Devon raised his hand. "How do we know which promises go where?"

Victor smiled. "We're about to find out."

He grabbed a stack of sticky notes and tossed them on the table.

"This afternoon," he said, "we're running a Drift Audit. We're going to surface every promise your company makes: written, spoken, implied, automated, or hallucinated."

Theo's eyes widened. "Every promise?"

"Every. Single. One."

The room suddenly felt smaller.

Because they all knew what was coming.

The truth was about to get messy.

TEN
THE PROMISE GATE

Before they started the audit, Victor held up his hand.

"One more thing," he said.

He wrote on the board:

THE PROMISE GATE

"What's that?" Rina asked.

"It's how you stop new drift from happening," Victor said. "It's the check-point every new promise has to pass through before it reaches a customer."

He drew three boxes:

CAN WE?

SHOULD WE?

WILL WE?

"Three questions," Victor said. "Every new promise, every claim, every feature, every message has to pass all three before it goes public."

CAN WE? — Feasibility. Is this technically, operationally, logistically possible *today*?

SHOULD WE? — Alignment. Does this reinforce our Core Promise or dilute it?

WILL WE? — Commitment. Can we deliver this *every time*, without heroics, across our entire team?

"If the answer to any of these is no," Victor said, "the promise doesn't go out. Period."

Theo leaned back. "So you're saying Sales needs... permission to make promises?"

Victor met his eyes. "I'm saying Sales needs *protection* from making promises the company can't keep."

Theo's jaw tightened. "That's going to slow us down."

"No," Victor said calmly. "It's going to stop you from promising things that create problems six months later."

The two men stared at each other.

Marcus jumped in. "Theo, think about it. How many deals have we won that turned into nightmares because we overpromised?"

Theo didn't answer right away.

"A few," he finally admitted.

"More than a few," Tessa said quietly.

Theo shot her a look. But he didn't argue.

"Here's how it works," Victor continued. "You form a Gate Committee. Three to five people. Cross-functional. Delivery, Support, Sales, Product, Marketing."

"Their job is to evaluate every new promise before it escapes into the wild."

He pointed to Rina. "If Marketing wants to launch a new campaign with new claims, it goes through the Gate."

He pointed to Theo. "If Sales wants to add a new feature to the pitch deck, it goes through the Gate."

He pointed to the empty chair where Product usually sat. "If Product wants to beta test something with customers, it goes through the Gate."

"Nothing gets out," Victor said, "until it passes all three questions."

Devon raised his hand. "What if something's already out there? Like the AI chatbot making promises we didn't approve?"

Victor smiled grimly. "Then you audit it. You find every promise it's making. And you either make it real—or you kill it."

He capped the marker.

"That's what we're about to do."

The Drift Audit was next.

And no one was ready for what they'd find.

ELEVEN
THE DRIFT AUDIT

The team walked into the conference room the next morning with coffee in hand and dread in their hearts.

They knew today would be uncomfortable.

Victor greeted them with his usual calm, but Marcus noticed something in his eyes. Anticipation? Nervousness?

"Morning," Victor said. "Today we surface every promise your company makes—intentionally or not."

Theo muttered under his breath: "Buckle up."

Victor stepped to the whiteboard and wrote in large letters:

THE DRIFT AUDIT

All the Promises You Didn't Know You Were Making

He turned to them. "Most companies believe they make twenty to thirty promises. In reality, it's usually hundreds."

Rina's eyes widened. "That can't be right."

Victor smiled kindly. "Let's find out."

He handed out thick stacks of sticky notes and markers.

"We'll start with one question," he said, writing it on the board:

"What does a customer expect from us the moment they say yes?"

He pointed to the sticky notes.

"Every answer gets its own note. No debate. No judgment. No filtering. Just truth.

Stage 1: The Surface Promises

At first, the notes came slowly. Carefully.

- "Reliable workflows"
- "Clean onboarding"
- "Quick support responses"
- "Clear communication"
- "Accurate documentation"

Simple. Predictable. Safe.

Victor nodded as they stuck them to the wall. "Good. That's the surface."

Then the next layer started.

- "A demo that matches reality"
- "Integration without surprises"
- "A stable AI agent"
- "Delivery that stays on timeline"
- "No unexpected costs"

The wall started filling.

Victor stepped back. "Now we're getting closer."

Stage 2: The Hidden Promises

Then something shifted.

Devon wrote on a sticky: **"Support won't contradict Sales."**

He stuck it to the wall without looking at Theo.

Theo frowned. "Hey—"

Victor held up a hand. "No debating. Truth only."

Rina added: **"Marketing won't oversell features."**

Tessa wrote: **"Delivery can fix whatever was promised."**

More notes followed:

- "Offshore teams know what we offer"
- "The AI bot understands our product"
- "Documentation reflects current reality"
- "Customer success knows what's on the roadmap"

Marcus wrote one that made the room go silent:

"We'll make their world simpler, not more confusing."

Victor nodded slowly. "This is the heart of your brand. And the first thing to break when drift begins."

He motioned for them to keep going.

Stage 3: The Accidental Promises

This is where things got messy.

Rina added: **"If it's on our website, it's true."**

Theo added: **"If I say 'yes,' the company backs me up."**

Tessa added: **"If Product experimented with it once, customers think it exists."**

Devon added: **"If the AI bot says it, customers assume it's official."**

One of the team members in the back—a customer success manager—added quietly:

"If I mention a future idea in a check-in call, customers treat it like a guarantee."

The stickies now covered half the wall.

Victor stood back, arms crossed, studying the mosaic.

"These," he said, pointing, "are the promises causing drift. Because no one is guarding them."

Stage 4: The Legacy Promises

Victor wrote on the board:

LEGACY PROMISES = Promises that outlived their truth

"Now," he said, "the hardest layer."

Tessa went first.

She picked up a sticky and wrote with a grimace:

"We integrate with anything."

Theo groaned. "That was *one campaign*. Three years ago."

"But people still believe it," Tessa said.

Next came a flood:

- "Onboarding takes three weeks" (*It hadn't for years*)
- "Support is 24/7" (*It never was*)
- "Unlimited automations" (*Marketing mistake from 2019*)
- "Plug-and-play integrations" (*Never existed*)
- "Smart workflows that learn automatically" (*Old prototype*)
- "Predictive scheduling" (*AI hallucination based on old copy*)

Rina covered her face with her hands. "I can't believe some of these are still alive."

Victor nodded grimly. "Legacy promises don't disappear. They fossilize. And customers dig them up."

By the time they were done, the walls of the conference room were covered, floor to ceiling, with hundreds of sticky notes.

A mosaic of truth.

A map of drift.

A mirror no one had expected to be this honest.

Victor stood in the center of the room, slowly turning in a circle, taking it all in.

"This," he said quietly, "is your company's promise ecosystem."

He stepped closer to the wall.

"Every one of these came from somewhere. A sales conversation. A bot. A demo. A slide. A feature. A rumor. A memory. An assumption."

He turned to face them.

"And all of them, together, define what your customers expect from you."

The silence was heavy.

Marcus finally spoke, his voice barely above a whisper.

"No wonder our teams are overwhelmed."

"Exactly," Victor said. "Your people are doing *heroic* work trying to keep promises the company never intended to make."

He took a breath.

"Tomorrow, we sort these into your Stack. And for the first time, you'll see which promises belong in your future... and which ones must be retired."

His tone softened.

"This is the beginning of alignment."

And for the first time all week, no one in the room doubted him.

TWELVE
REWRITING THE STACK

The next morning, the conference room looked like a crime scene investigation.

The sticky notes from yesterday still covered three walls, hundreds of them, a colorful collage of every promise the company had ever made, intentionally or not.

Today, they weren't just going to look at the mess.

They were going to clean it up.

Victor stood at the far end of the room, hands in his pockets, studying the wall like an archaeologist examining artifacts.

"This," he said, sweeping a hand toward the chaos, "is your past."

He turned to face them.

"Today we build your future."

Step 1: Sort the Promises

Victor handed out colored markers.

"Every promise goes into one of five categories from your Promise Stack."

He wrote them on a clean section of whiteboard:

1. **CORE PROMISE** (*Only ONE*)

2. **SUPPORTING PROMISES** (*Must work for Core to work*)

3. **CONDITIONAL PROMISES** (*Real, but only under specific conditions*)

4. **EXPERIMENTAL PROMISES** (*Not ready for customers yet*)

5. **LEGACY PROMISES** (*Need to be killed*)

"Only one promise belongs in Core," Victor said, pointing to the top. "Everything else either supports it, conditions it, or distracts from it."

They began sorting.

At first, it went quickly.

- "We simplify complex workflows so they're immediately clear" → **CORE**
- "Accurate documentation" → **SUPPORTING**
- "Clear onboarding" → **SUPPORTING**
- "Responsive support" → **SUPPORTING**
- "Custom workflows" → **CONDITIONAL** (only on Enterprise plan)
- "Advanced integrations" → **CONDITIONAL** (only with standard APIs)
- "Beta AI task suggestions" → **EXPERIMENTAL**

But quickly, the sorting became harder.

Much harder.

"What about 'fast response times'?" Devon asked, holding up a sticky.

Victor raised an eyebrow. "Do you deliver that *every time*?"

Devon hesitated. "No. We try. But volume spikes—"

"Conditional, then," Victor said. "Not a guarantee."

Devon moved it to the Conditional column.

Rina held up another sticky: **"Improving operational efficiency."**

Victor pointed at the Core Promise on the board.

"That's an outcome, not a promise. If workflows are clear, efficiency *might* improve. But you can't control that."

He shook his head. "Not a promise."

Rina crumpled the sticky and tossed it in the trash.

Theo groaned as he held up a note: **"Advanced automation for predictive scheduling."**

"We don't even have this anymore," he said. "Customers still ask for it."

"Legacy," Victor said without pausing. "Sunset it officially. Communicate it clearly."

Theo moved it to the Legacy column with a grimace.

They continued for hours.

Sorting.

Debating.

Re-evaluating.

Confronting truths they'd been avoiding.

Tessa challenged Victor on whether "24-hour onboarding" was Supporting or Conditional.

"Can you deliver it every time?" Victor asked.

"If the customer shows up prepared with clean data... yes."

"Then it's Conditional," Victor said. "The promise depends on something outside your control."

Tessa moved it.

By lunchtime, the walls looked different—organized, categorized, clearer.

The weight in the room had lifted. Slightly.

They were beginning to see themselves again.

Step 2: Decide What Stays—and What Dies

After lunch, Victor walked to the Legacy Promises section.

There were at least forty sticky notes there.

He drew a large red "X" through the entire section.

"These," he said, "are the promises hurting your business."

He turned to face them.

"Some can be retired quietly. Others need to be killed publicly and clearly, so customers know they're gone."

Rina picked up one: **"Unlimited automations."**

"This needs a public sunset announcement," she said. "People still mention it in reviews."

Victor nodded. "Write an email. Update the FAQ. Train Support to handle questions. Make it clear."

Theo held up another: **"We integrate with anything."**

"Same," Victor said. "Public correction. 'We integrate with systems using standard APIs. Here's the list of supported platforms.'"

Theo made a note.

Devon pointed at **"24/7 support."**

"We never had this," he said. "But somehow people think we do."

"Update your website," Victor said. "Make support hours visible. Train offshore to clarify when they're online."

Devon nodded.

One by one, they went through the Legacy column.

Killing promises.

Clarifying reality.

Setting the record straight.

It felt brutal.

But also... freeing.

Step 3: Define the Boundaries

Victor pointed to the Conditional Promises section.

"These are dangerous," he said. "Because they're real promises—but only sometimes."

He wrote on the board:

CONDITIONAL PROMISES MUST HAVE CLEAR CONDITIONS

"If you promise custom workflows on Enterprise plans," Victor said, "every customer-facing person needs to know that. Sales. Support. Onboarding. AI. Everyone."

He pointed to Rina. "And it needs to be in your messaging. 'Custom workflows available on Enterprise plans.' Not 'We offer custom workflows.'"

Rina made a note.

"Same with integrations," Victor continued. "If you only integrate with standard APIs, SAY THAT. Don't let people assume you integrate with everything."

Theo nodded.

"And if you offer fast onboarding only when customers show up prepared, SAY THAT. Set the expectation up front."

Tessa was nodding. "So we're being honest about conditions."

"Exactly," Victor said. "Conditional Promises aren't bad. But they have to be *clearly* conditional."

Step 4: Protect the Core

Victor stood in front of the Core Promise:

"We simplify complex workflows so they're immediately clear."

"This," he said, tapping the board, "is sacred. Everything you do either protects this promise or threatens it."

He turned to them.

"Every new feature. Every new message. Every new claim. Before it goes out, ask: Does this make workflows *clearer*? Or does it make things more complex?"

"If it makes things more complex," Victor said firmly, "it doesn't belong."

The room was quiet.

Marcus spoke first. "So we're saying no to things that don't align."

"Yes," Victor said.

"Even if they'd make us money?"

"*Especially* if they'd make you money," Victor replied. "Because misaligned promises destroy trust. And trust is worth more than any single deal."

Theo shifted uncomfortably. But he didn't argue.

By the end of the day, the wall looked different.

Organized. Clear. Honest.

Five distinct sections:

CORE — One promise

SUPPORTING — Twelve promises that enable the Core

CONDITIONAL — Eight promises with clear conditions

EXPERIMENTAL — Five features still being tested

LEGACY — Forty-two promises being retired

Victor stood back, arms crossed, studying the work.

"This," he said quietly, "is your Promise Stack."

He turned to face them.

"This is who you are. This is what you promise. This is what you keep."

The team stared at the wall.

For the first time all week, they saw themselves clearly.

Marcus broke the silence. "What's next?"

Victor smiled. And this time, the confidence was real.

"Next," he said, "we build the systems to protect this. The Gate. The Rhythm. The Alignment Network."

He capped his marker.

"But first, we celebrate."

Rina looked up, surprised. "Celebrate?"

"You just did the hardest part," Victor said. "You told the truth."

He looked around the room.

"That's worth celebrating."

And for the first time in weeks, the team allowed themselves to feel something they hadn't felt in a long time:

Hope.

THIRTEEN

THE GLOBAL TEAM SPEAKS UP

Victor arrived early the next morning with a request that surprised Marcus.

"I need to talk to your offshore teams," he said. "Alone, first. Then with you."

Marcus hesitated. "Why alone?"

"Because," Victor said, "they won't tell you the truth if you're in the room. Not yet."

That stung. But Marcus knew Victor was right.

"Okay," he said. "Set it up."

———

An hour later, Victor sat in the conference room with just a laptop. The screen flickered to life.

Five faces appeared. Manila. Bogotá. Late evening for them. They looked tired. Curious. Wary.

A woman named Maria, support lead in Manila, spoke first.

"Is there... a problem?" Her voice was careful.

"No," Victor said gently. "I just need to understand what you see. What your reality is like."

Long pause.

Then Paolo, from Bogotá, leaned toward his camera.

"You really want to know?"

"I really want to know."

Paolo exhaled. "Okay. We see everything *last*. After promises break. After customers are angry. After things have already gone wrong."

Victor nodded. "Tell me more."

The Truth They'd Been Holding

Maria spoke next. Her voice was quiet but firm.

"Customers send us screenshots of chatbot responses. Features we've never heard of. Workflows that don't exist. And when we say 'we don't have that,' they think *we're* lying."

Aina, another team member, added: "Sometimes we follow documentation that turns out to be outdated. No one tells us it changed. We give the wrong answer. Customers get angry. We look incompetent."

Paolo's jaw tightened. "We've had to add two extra shifts just to handle escalations. We're staffing nights and weekends now because the volume keeps growing. Every confused customer becomes an escalation. Every mismatch between what they expect and what we deliver becomes our problem."

Maria nodded. "We've doubled our team size in six months. Not because business is growing—because confusion is growing. We're hiring people just to handle the mess."

"And we still can't keep up," Paolo added quietly. "Because we're guessing half the time."

"Guessing about what?" Victor asked.

"What's real," Paolo said. "What's current. What we're actually supposed to tell customers."

The silence that followed was heavy.

Then Maria said something that made Victor's chest tighten:

"We're not weak links. We're strong links working with unclear information."

Victor wrote that down. Word for word.

"Thank you," he said. "That's exactly what I needed to hear."

Bringing Leadership In

Twenty minutes later, the AxisLine leadership team joined the call.

The offshore team's body language shifted immediately. More guarded. More polished.

Victor noticed.

"We're not here to blame anyone," he said. "We're here to fix what's broken."

He turned to Maria. "Can you tell them what you told me? About the screenshots?"

Maria hesitated. Glanced at Marcus.

Marcus leaned forward. "Please. We need to hear it."

She told them. About the chatbot promising features that didn't exist. About documentation that contradicted itself. About doubling the team size just to handle the confusion. About adding night and weekend shifts for escalations.

Devon's shoulders slumped.

Theo rubbed his forehead.

Rina looked like she might cry.

When Paolo mentioned staffing two extra shifts just to handle the mess, Tessa actually did.

"I had no idea," she whispered.

"We didn't want to complain," Aina said quickly. "We just wanted to do our jobs well."

Victor let the silence sit.

Then Marcus spoke, his voice thick.

"You've been carrying our mess. And we didn't even know. I'm sorry."

Maria blinked, surprised. "Thank you for saying that."

"It's not enough," Marcus said. "But it's a start."

Victor turned to the leadership team.

"This," he said quietly, "is the human cost of drift. Your offshore teams aren't an afterthought. They're essential to keeping your company aligned."

He looked back at the screen.

"But they can't do that if they're working in the dark."

Marcus stepped forward. He'd been quiet through most of the call, absorbing what he'd heard. Now he knew what needed to happen.

"Maria, Paolo, Aina—everyone on your teams," he said. "We're bringing you into the system we're building. It's called the Promise Alignment System."

He glanced at Victor, who nodded encouragingly.

"Over the next two weeks, we're going to train you on everything. The Core Promise. The Promise Stack—how we categorize what we offer. The Promise Gate—how we decide what gets promised. Our Alignment Rhythm—the weekly meetings where we catch problems early."

Maria's eyes widened. "You want us... in leadership meetings?"

"Not just in them," Marcus said. "You'll be running some of them. You see drift before anyone else does. You catch mismatches between what customers expect and what we deliver. That makes you critical to the system, not optional."

He leaned toward the camera.

"Starting next week, you'll have someone from my team—probably Tessa or Devon—walk you through the framework. Two training sessions, one hour each. Then you'll be part of our weekly Standup. You'll see Stack updates in real time. You'll have access to the same documentation, the same truth, the same system everyone else uses."

Paolo looked stunned. "We've never been included like this before."

"I know," Marcus said. "That was our mistake. We're fixing it."

Aina spoke up hesitantly. "What if we see something wrong? Can we... say something?"

"You don't just *can*," Marcus said firmly. "You *should*. If you spot drift—if something doesn't match the Stack, if a customer mentions a feature we don't have, if documentation is wrong—you flag it immediately. No hierarchy. No permission needed. You see it, you say it."

Maria sat back, processing this.

"This is..." She paused. "This is different."

"It has to be," Marcus said. "We've been operating like you're support staff. But you're not. You're part of the team that keeps our word to customers. And that means you need the same tools, the same information, and the same voice as everyone else."

"Really?" Maria asked, her voice softer now.

"Really," Marcus said.

The call ended a few minutes later.

When the screen went dark, no one spoke for a long time.

Finally, Tessa broke the silence.

"We can't ever go back to how things were."

"No," Marcus agreed. "We can't."

FOURTEEN
THE FIRST FAILURES

The next two weeks were brutal.

Not because the work was hard—though it was. But because *nothing worked the first time.*

Failure #1: The AI Keeps Hallucinating

Devon's team spent three days retraining the chatbot on the new Promise Stack.

They stripped out all the old training data. Fed it only current, Gate-approved information. Set strict guardrails.

Then they tested it.

Customer: "Do you offer predictive scheduling?"

Bot: "Our system includes advanced workflow capabilities that can help with scheduling optimization."

Devon stared at the screen.

"That's still a yes," he said flatly. "It's just a *vague* yes."

They tried again. Tightened the prompts. Added more constraints.

Customer: "Can you integrate with SAP?"

Bot: "We support integrations with enterprise systems through our API framework."

"It's *implying* yes without saying yes," Rina said, frustrated. "That's worse."

Third attempt. This time they gave the bot explicit "NO" scripts.

Customer: "Do you offer predictive scheduling?"

Bot: "No, we do not currently offer predictive scheduling. However, our workflow automation can help streamline scheduling processes."

"Better," Victor said. "But it's still adding features at the end. The 'however' creates drift."

It took eleven iterations before the bot could give a clean answer:

Customer: "Do you offer predictive scheduling?"

Bot: "No, we don't offer predictive scheduling. Our platform simplifies complex workflows so they're immediately clear. Would you like to know more about our core capabilities?"

Devon exhaled. "Finally."

"Now do that for every feature," Victor said.

Devon groaned.

Failure #2: Sales Rebels Against the Gate

Theo called a sales team meeting to explain the new Promise Gate.

It did not go well.

"So let me get this straight," one of his top reps said, arms crossed. "I need to get *approval* before adding features to my pitch deck?"

"Not approval," Theo said. "Validation. To make sure what you're promising is real."

"I've been selling for eight years. I know what's real."

"Do you?" Theo asked, more sharply than he intended. "Because we've been promising 'advanced integrations' to customers who then find out it only works with three specific systems."

The rep's face reddened. "That's Product's fault for not building it."

"No," Theo said. "That's *our* fault for promising it before checking."

Another rep jumped in. "This is going to kill our close rate."

"You know what else kills close rates?" Theo shot back. "Angry customers who churn because we overpromised."

The meeting ended with half the sales team storming out.

Theo sat alone in the conference room afterward, head in his hands.

Marcus found him there twenty minutes later.

"They hate me," Theo said.

"They'll get over it," Marcus replied. "Or they won't. Either way, we're doing this."

"What if they're right? What if this kills sales?"

Marcus sat down. "Then we'll figure it out. But we're not going back."

Failure #3: The First Weekly Standup Is a Disaster

The first Weekly Promise Standup was supposed to take 15 minutes.

It took 90.

Everyone brought "drift sightings"—but no one could agree on what counted as drift.

"A customer asked about custom dashboards," Devon said. "Is that drift?"

"Did we promise custom dashboards?" Victor asked.

"Not explicitly. But our marketing says 'customizable.'"

"That's different," Rina argued. "Customizable means they can configure settings. It doesn't mean custom-built."

"But customers interpret it that way," Tessa said.

"Then it's drift," Victor said. "If customers expect it and we didn't intend it, that's drift."

They went in circles like this for an hour.

By the end, everyone was exhausted.

"This is never going to work," Theo muttered.

Victor heard him. "It will. But not today."

<hr>

The Breaking Point

Two and a half weeks in, Marcus called an emergency meeting.

"We need to talk," he said. The team filed in, looking tired.

"I know this has been hard," Marcus started.

"Hard?" Theo interrupted. "Marcus, my team is in open revolt. Half of them think we've lost our minds."

"Delivery is drowning," Tessa added. "We're rewriting documentation, updating onboarding, and trying to hit our normal targets. Something's going to break."

Devon raised his hand. "Support ticket volume is actually *up*. Customers are confused by the changes."

Rina looked miserable. "Marketing put out new messaging last week. Three customers emailed asking if we're pivoting our product."

Marcus looked at Victor. "Are we doing this wrong?"

Victor was quiet for a moment.

Then he stood up.

"No," he said. "You're doing it exactly right."

Everyone stared at him.

"Change is *supposed* to be messy," Victor continued. "You're not failing. You're learning. The AI hallucinated—so you learned how to constrain it better. Sales pushed back—so you learned what training they need. The Standup took too long—so you'll get faster."

He walked to the whiteboard.

"You've been drifting for *years*. Did you think you'd fix it in two weeks?"

Silence.

"How long will this take?" Marcus asked quietly.

Victor met his eyes. "Three months. Minimum. And it's going to be hard the whole way."

Tessa laughed—the kind without humor. "Great."

"But," Victor added, "if you quit now, you go back to what you were. And that was killing you."

He capped the marker.

"So the question is: Are you willing to stay uncomfortable long enough to become something better?"

Marcus looked around the table.

Theo. Still frustrated, but nodding.

Tessa. Exhausted, but not giving up.

Devon. Tired, but resolute.

Rina. Worried, but committed.

"Yeah," Marcus said. "We're willing."

Victor smiled. "Good. Because it gets worse before it gets better."

Everyone groaned.

But no one left.

FIFTEEN
VICTOR'S TRANSITION

Six weeks in, Victor pulled Marcus aside after a Standup.

"We need to talk about what happens next," he said.

Marcus's stomach dropped. "You're leaving?"

"Not exactly," Victor said. "But my role needs to change."

He gestured to the room where the team was still debating a drift sighting.

"Look at them. They're running the Standups. They're using the Gate. They're catching drift. They're making decisions. They don't need me in the room every day anymore."

"But there's still so much—"

"There will *always* be more," Victor interrupted gently. "That's the point. This isn't a project with an end date. It's an operating system. And you need to run it without me hovering."

Marcus sat down heavily.

"What if we screw it up?"

Victor smiled. "You will. Multiple times. But you'll also fix it. Because you know how now."

Victor was quiet for a moment after he said it.

Marcus watched him. In six weeks, he'd seen Victor uncertain once — the morning of the Core Promise session, when he'd admitted "I don't know yet" and sat down facing the team instead of the whiteboard. That moment had made Marcus trust him more than anything else.

This felt like the same thing. Not doubt. Something quieter than doubt.

"You okay?" Marcus asked.

Victor looked up. Almost surprised by the question.

"Yeah," he said. And then, after a beat: "I've done this enough times to know which companies make it and which ones don't. The ones that don't — they're not bad companies. They're just not willing to be uncomfortable long enough."

He glanced back toward the conference room.

"You're willing. That's rarer than you think."

He picked up his notebook.

The New Structure

Victor pulled out his notebook.

"Here's what I'm proposing," he said. "I stop coming to weekly Standups. You run those. Tessa, Devon, whoever—you rotate the facilitation. No more relying on me to keep you on track."

Marcus nodded slowly.

"But," Victor continued, "I come back quarterly. We do a full-day Quarterly Alignment Review. Deep dive on the Stack. Look at what's working, what's drifting, what needs to change. I help you course-correct, but you do the daily work."

He flipped the page.

"In lieu of one of the Quarterly Reviews, we do an annual two-day Strategic Alignment Session. Review your Core Promise. Assess if it still fits. Update the Stack for new products or market changes. Make sure your system is evolving with your business."

"So you're not *leaving* leaving," Marcus said.

"I'm transitioning," Victor replied. "From daily partner to quarterly advisor. You need to own this system. I need to make sure you can."

Marcus took a breath. "When does this start?"

"Next week," Victor said. "Your team runs the next Standup. I'll watch, but I won't step in unless something's seriously off track."

"And if we fail?"

"Then we'll fix it in the quarterly review," Victor said. "But you won't fail. You're ready."

The Final Daily Standup

Victor's last daily Standup was a Friday.

No big announcement. He just sat in the back instead of leading from the front.

Tessa ran the meeting. Started nervous, but found her rhythm.

When someone asked Victor a question, he looked at Tessa.

"What do you think?" he asked.

She thought for a moment. Then answered. Correctly.

By the end of the meeting, no one was looking at Victor anymore. They were looking at each other.

When it ended, Victor stood up quietly and headed for the door.

Marcus caught him in the hallway.

"That was harder than I expected," Marcus admitted. "Watching you just... sit there."

"Good," Victor said. "That means you're taking ownership."

He extended his hand.

"See you in three months for the Quarterly Review. And call me if something urgent comes up. But otherwise..." He smiled. "You've got this."

Marcus shook his hand. "Thanks. For everything."

"You did the work," Victor replied. "I just showed you the system."

Then he walked out.

Marcus stood there for a moment. The panic he'd expected didn't come.

Instead, he felt something else: readiness.

He turned and headed back to the conference room where Tessa was already setting up for a Stack review.

"Ready?" she asked.

"Ready," Marcus said.

And they continued.

That night, Victor sat in his car in the parking garage for a few minutes before driving home.

He opened his notebook to a fresh page. Wrote three names at the top — his next three clients. Companies in different industries, different sizes, different failure modes. But the same underlying problem: promises proliferating faster than anyone was managing them.

He thought about AxisLine. About Tessa running the Standup. About Marcus standing in the hallway saying *that was harder than I expected.*

He closed the notebook.

The question he always asked himself at moments like this wasn't *did they make it?* — he wouldn't know that for months yet. The question was simpler: *Are they willing to keep going when I'm not in the room?*

He'd seen the answer today.

He started the car and pulled out of the garage.

SIXTEEN
THE SLOW CLIMB BACK

The first month without Victor was rough. Really rough.

Week 1: The Wobble

The first Standup without Victor went long again. They got bogged down in details, forgot to track action items, and ended without clear next steps.

"That was a disaster," Tessa said afterward.

"Yeah," Marcus agreed. "But we'll be better next week."

They were. A little.

Week 3: Sales Starts to See It

One of Theo's reps—the one who'd stormed out of the Gate meeting—came back with a confession.

"I closed a deal last week using only Gate-approved features," she said. "Customer asked about predictive scheduling. I said no. Explained what we *actually* do."

"And?" Theo asked.

"They signed anyway. Said they appreciated the honesty. It was... weird. But good weird."

Theo smiled. "That's the point."

Over the next two weeks, three more reps had similar stories. The rebellion was ending.

Week 5: The First Clean Drift Audit

The Monthly Stack Review finally clicked.

They identified four new Conditional Promises that needed clarification.

They found two Legacy Promises still floating around.

They caught three Experimental features that had leaked into demo decks.

And they fixed all of them.

In one meeting.

"We're getting good at this," Devon said.

"We're getting *better*," Marcus corrected. "We're not good yet."

But they were improving. Steadily.

Week 8: Offshore Team Flags
a Problem Before It Escalates

Maria from Manila pinged the leadership channel at 10 PM PST (10 AM Manila time).

"FYI - Three customers today asked about 'hyper-flex automation.' Not sure where that's coming from but it's not in our Stack. Might want to check."

Rina did a quick search. Found it in a LinkedIn ad that hadn't been updated. Killed it within the hour.

"This," Marcus said in the next Standup, "is what success looks like. Catching drift *before* it spreads."

The whole team felt it. They were actually getting ahead of problems instead of chasing them.

SEVENTEEN
THE TURNAROUND

Three months after Victor left, something shifted. The wins started coming faster.

Win #1: NPS Climbs

Devon walked into the leadership meeting with a printout.

"Look at this."

NPS: 27 → 41

"In three months," he said. "Customers are noticing."

The comments told the story:

"AxisLine finally feels clear about what they do."

"No more surprises. I actually know what I'm getting."

"Support and Sales are saying the same thing now. It's refreshing."

Rina's eyes welled up. "We did that."

"Yeah," Marcus said. "We did."

Win #2: Offshore Team Celebrates

The monthly all-hands call with the offshore teams had a different energy.

Paolo spoke up: "We wanted to say thank you. The new documentation is clear. The Stack updates are immediate. We're not guessing anymore."

Aina added: "And the escalations? They're down. Way down. We haven't had to add any new shifts in two months. Actually thinking about reducing back to our core team."

Maria smiled into the camera. "We feel like part of the team now. Not just... the cleanup crew."

Marcus felt the weight of that.

"You *are* part of the team," he said. "And we should've made that clear from day one."

Win #3: Theo's Team Buys In

The sales team meeting was different this time.

No arms crossed. No storming out.

One rep raised her hand. "Can we add the Gate checklist to our CRM? So it auto-checks promises before we send proposals?"

Theo blinked. "You... *want* that?"

"Yeah. It's actually helpful. Keeps us from overpromising."

Another rep added: "My close rate's up 12% this quarter. Turns out honesty works."

Theo looked at Marcus. Shook his head in disbelief.

"They're bought in," he said later. "Actually bought in."

Win #4: The AI Finally Works

Devon demoed the retrained chatbot in a leadership meeting.

Customer: "Do you offer 24/7 support?"

Bot: "Our support team is available Monday-Friday, 6 AM - 10 PM PST. For urgent issues outside those hours, you can submit a ticket and we'll respond first thing the next business day."

Customer: "Can you integrate with my custom ERP system?"

Bot: "We integrate with systems that use standard REST APIs. If your ERP supports that, we can likely integrate. Want to schedule a technical call to confirm compatibility?"

Clean. Clear. Honest.

"It took four months," Devon said. "But it finally works."

"It was worth it," Rina said.

Win #5: The Moment They Knew

The proof came in the form of a renewal.

Their hardest customer. The one who'd been threatening to churn for months. The one who'd complained endlessly about inconsistency.

They renewed. Early. And upgraded to Enterprise.

The note from their CEO said:

"Whatever you did over the last few months, keep doing it. AxisLine feels like a completely different company. Clear. Reliable. Trustworthy. That's worth paying for."

Marcus read it aloud in the leadership meeting.

When he finished, the room was silent.

Then Tessa started clapping.

Then everyone else joined.

Not because they'd won a deal.

Because they'd earned it.

EIGHTEEN
THE NEW IDENTITY

Four months after Victor's transition, Marcus called a different kind of meeting.

"We need to talk about who we are now," he said.

The team settled in. Victor was on the screen—joining remotely for their first Quarterly Alignment Review since transitioning to advisor.

"When I first got here," Victor said from the video call, "you were drifting. You didn't know what you stood for. You were making hundreds of promises and keeping none of them well."

He leaned toward his camera.

"You're not that company anymore. So the question is: who are you now?"

Defining the New Identity

Tessa spoke first. "We're clear now. That's the biggest change."

Devon nodded. "We're consistent. Customers actually know what to expect."

Rina added: "We're honest. We don't overpromise."

Theo surprised everyone by saying: "We're disciplined. We have systems that keep us aligned."

Marcus wrote on the whiteboard:

Clear. Consistent. Honest. Disciplined.

"Those are good," he said. "But what ties them together?"

The room went quiet.

Then Tessa said it: "We keep our word."

Everyone turned to look at her.

"That's who we are now," she said. "The company that keeps its word."

Marcus wrote it on the board:

THE COMPANY THAT KEEPS ITS WORD

It sat there. Simple. True. Powerful.

"That's it," Rina whispered. "That's us."

The Culture Shift

"I've noticed something," Devon said. "People are... different. Calmer. More confident."

Tessa agreed. "My team isn't scrambling anymore. They know what they're responsible for keeping. They're not trying to save promises they didn't make."

Theo nodded. "Sales isn't guessing. They know exactly what they can promise. It's actually easier."

"And offshore?" Marcus asked.

"They're part of the team now," Devon said. "Actually part of it. They catch drift. They flag problems. They're not just cleaning up our mess."

Marcus felt it too. The office felt different. Lighter. More focused.

"This is what alignment feels like," he said.

NINETEEN
THE PROMISE COMPANY

Six months after Victor first walked through the doors, AxisLine had become something different. Not perfect. But fundamentally changed.

The Numbers

Marcus presented to the board:

NPS: 27 → 48

Customer Retention: +18%

Support Tickets: -31%

Sales Cycle: -2 weeks (faster)

Offshore Team Efficiency: Reduced from 6 shifts back to 4 (eliminated the extra shifts added to handle escalations)

"How?" one board member asked.

"We stopped drifting," Marcus said simply. "We defined our Core Promise. We built a Stack. We installed a Gate. We run a weekly Alignment Rhythm. And we made our entire team—human and AI—Promise Keepers."

He clicked to the next slide.

CORE PROMISE: *"We simplify complex workflows so they're immediately clear."*

"That's it," he said. "That's what we keep. Every time. No exceptions."

The board member leaned back. "And it's working?"

Marcus smiled. "It's working."

What They Became

AxisLine wasn't the fastest-growing company.

Or the flashiest.

Or the most aggressive.

But they were becoming something rarer:

A company people trusted.

Customers renewed because they knew what to expect.

Employees stayed because they weren't set up to fail.

The offshore team felt valued instead of isolated.

Sales closed deals with honesty instead of hype.

And it showed.

In the comments customers left:

"AxisLine doesn't overpromise. That's so rare."

"They're clear about what they can and can't do. I respect that."

"Finally, a company that means what it says."

The Final Scene

One Tuesday morning, Marcus walked through the office.

He noticed things:

Jasmine, the onboarding specialist who'd been drowning six months ago, laughing with a customer on a call.

The support team's dashboard showing green across the board.

A sales rep using the Promise Gate checklist before sending a proposal.

The offshore team's Slack channel filled with helpful updates instead of panicked questions at 3 AM.

He stopped at the mission statement on the wall:

~~Empowering teams with intelligent workflows.~~

Someone had put a sticky note over it:

The company that keeps its word.

Marcus smiled.

Then he headed to the conference room for the Weekly Promise Standup.

Tessa was already there, pulling up the agenda.

"Ready?" she asked.

"Ready," Marcus said.

And they began.

The work did not end there.

Drift still happened.

But now they had a system to catch it.

They had a rhythm to correct it.

They had a network aligned to stop it.

And every quarter, they had Victor to help them course-correct where needed.

Most importantly: They had become a Promise Company.

EPILOGUE: THE QUARTERLY REVIEW

Victor walked into AxisLine's office on a Tuesday morning carrying his notebook and a coffee.

The receptionist smiled. "Welcome back, Victor. They're waiting for you in the conference room."

"Thanks, Jasmine," he said.

As he walked through the office, he noticed the changes.

The support dashboard on the wall showed mostly green.

The sales team's whiteboard had "Gate Approved" stickers on three new pitch decks.

Someone had updated the mission statement:

~~Empowering teams with intelligent workflows.~~

The company that keeps its word.

He smiled.

The leadership team was already assembled when he entered.

Marcus stood to greet him. "Good to see you."

"You too," Victor said. "How've the last three months been?"

"Hard," Tessa admitted. "But good."

"We had two major failures," Devon added. "Want to hear about them?"

"That's exactly what I'm here for," Victor said, sitting down.

For the next six hours, they walked through everything:

What worked:

- The weekly Standups had become efficient (down to 30 minutes from 90, which is acceptable progress during the implementation)
- The offshore team had caught three drift instances before they escalated
- NPS had climbed from 41 to 48
- Sales close rates were up, churn was down

What didn't work:

- They'd let a Conditional Promise slip into marketing copy without Gate review (caught it after two weeks, but it caused confusion)
- A new product manager had tried to add features without Stack approval (they had to have a hard conversation)

What they were stuck on:

- How to handle promises made by third-party integrations
- Whether to add a new tier to their pricing (and what promises that implied)

Victor listened. Asked questions. Made notes. Helped them think through the stuck points.

By the end of the day, they had:

- Updated three Stack entries
- Clarified two Conditional Promises
- Added a new Gate checkpoint for third-party integrations
- Made a decision on the pricing tier (with clear promise boundaries)

"This is what the quarterly review is for," Victor said. "Not to fix everything. Just to make sure you're asking the right questions, catching what you missed, and making adjustments where necessary to ensure you stay aligned."

Marcus walked him out at the end of the day.

"We're doing this, aren't we?" Marcus said. "Actually doing it."

"You are," Victor confirmed. "And you'll keep doing it. See you in three months."

He headed for the door, then turned back.

"Oh, and Marcus? You don't need me as much as you think. But I'm glad you keep me around anyway."

Marcus smiled. "So are we."

The work continued. But that was the point - alignment wasn't a destination. It was a practice.

Victor drove home that evening thinking about the companies he'd seen do this — and the ones he'd watched refuse to.

The ones who refused weren't bad companies. They weren't led by careless people. They were just unwilling to sit in the discomfort of looking honestly at the gap between what they said and what they delivered. So the gap stayed. And widened. And eventually, quietly, cost them more than they ever expected.

AxisLine had been willing.

That was the whole difference.

He thought about Marcus standing in the parking lot, asking *"We're doing this, aren't we? Actually doing it."* The note of surprise in his voice. As if he'd expected, somewhere along the way, to fail.

Most leaders do expect to fail. Not because they're weak — but because they've tried to fix drift before with the wrong tools. With better communication trainings. With new org charts. With culture initiatives. And watched the drift return anyway, because the promises were never addressed at the source.

EPILOGUE: THE QUARTERLY REVIEW

That's what PAS does. It goes to the source.

Victor set his notebook on the passenger seat. Inside were the names of the next three companies on his list — each one somewhere in the drift cycle, each one not yet knowing there was a way out.

There always was.

The question was never *can this be fixed?*

It was always: *Are you willing to start?*

THE PROMISE ALIGNMENT SYSTEM

PREFACE

Your Turn

Before you turn this page, take one honest moment.

Think about your company. Not the version in your deck or your investor update or your all-hands presentation. The real version. The one your delivery team sees at 9 PM when a customer is escalating. The one your offshore team navigates at 3 AM when documentation doesn't match reality. The one your sales reps improvise around when the pitch runs into something they can't quite promise.

Does any of that look familiar?

If it does, even a little, you're already in the story. You were in it before you opened this book. You just didn't have a name for it yet.

Now you do. It's called Promise Drift. And it has a fix.

Part 2 reads differently than Part 1. You've been watching. Now you're working. The chapters ahead aren't a re-explanation of AxisLine's story.

Each chapter gives you the steps, the frameworks, and the worksheets to install PAS from the ground up. You'll find tools for defining your Core Promise, mapping your Promise Stack, installing your Promise Gate, building your Alignment Rhythm and Network, running your first Drift Audit, and executing a 90-day roadmap to take you from where you are now to a company that keeps its word.

Three ways to use Part 2:

1- If you want a structured implementation, follow the chapters in order and use the 90-Day Roadmap in Chapter 8 as your guide.

2 - If you have a specific problem burning right now, such as your AI is making promises you didn't approve, your sales team is improvising, your offshore teams are working from outdated scripts — go directly to the chapter that matches it.

3- If you've already started building alignment and need a reference, use Part 2 as the operating manual you return to each quarter.

There's no wrong entry point. The only wrong move is finishing Part 1 and going back to business as usual.

One thing to hold before you begin:

AxisLine didn't fix everything at once. They fixed one thing, then another, then another. They had failures: the AI kept hallucinating for weeks, sales rebelled, the first Stack Review ran 90 minutes and resolved nothing. Victor told them it would take three months minimum, and it did. Probably longer, honestly, before it felt natural.

You won't be different. The system works, but only if you stay in it long enough for it to work.

What AxisLine had, the one thing that mattered more than the framework, was a leadership team willing to be honest about the gap. Willing to look at the wall of sticky notes and say: *we made all of these promises, and we can't keep most of them.* That moment of honesty was harder than any implementation step that followed.

So before the steps and the worksheets and the roadmap: just be honest about your promise gap.

That's where every Promise Company starts.

Let's build yours.

ONE
THE CORE PROMISE

In Part 1, Chapter 8 of the AxisLine story, Marcus and the AxisLine team spent hours trying to define their Core Promise. They kept gravitating toward aspirational statements—"Empowering teams with intelligent workflows"—that sounded impressive but meant nothing operationally. Victor kept pushing them back to reality: What do you actually guarantee? What can you deliver even on your worst day?

They discovered what most companies discover: **your Core Promise isn't about what you sell—it's about what you guarantee.** AxisLine sold workflow automation software with dozens of features, but their Core Promise became something simpler: "We simplify complex workflows so they're immediately clear."

That clarity changed everything. Suddenly, every decision had a North Star. Every promise could be tested against one question: Does this align with our Core Promise?

Most leadership teams, when they first try this exercise, make the same mistake Marcus's team made — they describe what they sell, not what they guarantee. Keep that in mind as you work through what follows.

What a Core Promise Is (and Isn't)

A Core Promise is the single outcome your company guarantees to deliver — consistently, reliably, and without heroics.

It is not:

- A mission statement ("We empower teams everywhere.")
- A value proposition ("The most innovative platform on the market.")
- A tagline ("Experience limitless workflows.")
- A strategy ("We focus on enterprise customers.")
- A feature list ("We automate everything.")

All of those may be useful in their own context. None of them are promises. They're ideas. Aspirations. Positioning.

A Core Promise is what you *actually deliver* — not what you hope to deliver, not what your best customers get on your best day, but what every customer can count on every time.

The test is simple: Can your delivery team, your support team, your offshore team, and your AI all keep this promise without extraordinary effort?

If the answer is no, it's not your Core Promise yet.

The Core Promise Formula

A strong Core Promise usually follows this pattern:

We [deliver/outcome] for [who] in a way that is [reliable/specific].

Here are examples across industries:

- Tech SaaS: "We simplify complex workflows so they're immediately clear."
- Retail / eCommerce: "We deliver quality products on time, without surprises."
- Experiential Retail: "We create memorable in-person experiences — consistently, safely, and skillfully."
- Real Estate: "We close transactions on schedule with clarity at every step."
- Healthcare Services: We provide accurate, timely care with zero guesswork."
- Professional Services: "We provide clear, actionable guidance grounded in proven systems."
- AI-Driven Companies: "We deliver accurate, aligned responses governed by real-world truths."

Notice what these have in common: each one focuses on an outcome, sets a clear expectation, avoids hype, and describes something the company can deliver consistently.

How to Find Your Core Promise

Step 1: Analyze What You Actually Deliver

Look at your last 6–12 months of customers. Not the best ones. Not the outliers. Not the "hero saves." The average customer.

What outcome did they consistently receive?

Step 2: Identify Your "Always" Statements

Ask your team:

- What do we always deliver, no matter the customer?
- What will we never compromise?
- What do our best customers appreciate the most?
- What outcomes are we confident we can deliver every single time?

Step 3: Remove Aspirations

If it's something you want to do someday but cannot do today — remove it. The Core Promise must be real. Not future-state. Not "once we hire three more engineers." Real, right now.

Step 4: Test for Heroics

You saw this in AxisLine's fable. Their delivery team was pulling late nights to compensate for a Core Promise that had never been reality-tested. When Victor asked what they could deliver "on their worst day," the team went quiet. The heroics test exposed the gap.

If keeping the promise requires late nights, custom work, favor-pulling, exceptions, oversized effort, or reliance on one superstar employee — it does not qualify.

The Core Promise must be deliverable without extraordinary effort. That's what makes it scalable. That's what makes it true.

Step 5: Confirm with Your Alignment Network

Your delivery team, support team, offshore team, AI systems, and documentation team must all say: *"Yes. We can deliver this. Every time."*

If they hesitate, your Core Promise isn't ready. Go back to Step 2.

This step is critical. Leadership teams often define Core Promises that sound right in the conference room but collapse in the field. The people who keep your promises must validate them.

What Changes When You Define Your Core Promise

Once your Core Promise is clear, it becomes a decision filter for everything:

- **Sales** knows the boundaries of what they can promise.
- **Marketing** has a message rooted in truth, not aspiration.
- **Product** can prioritize what strengthens the promise and deprioritize what doesn't.
- **Support** stops apologizing for mismatched expectations.
- **Offshore teams** stop guessing — they know what the company stands for.
- **AI systems** can be trained to a single source of truth.
- **Leadership** can make faster decisions through one lens: "Does this protect or dilute our Core Promise?"

The Core Promise is the anchor. Everything else in PAS builds from it. If this foundation is vague, everything drifts. If it's clear, everything aligns.

Common Challenges When Defining Your Core Promise

Defining your Core Promise is conceptually simple but operationally difficult. Here are the most common challenges companies face—and how to resolve them.

Challenge #1: Your Team Can't Agree on One Core Promise

What this looks like:

- Marketing wants: "Innovative solutions that transform how you work"
- Sales wants: "Fast implementation with immediate ROI"
- Delivery wants: "Reliable software that just works"
- Support wants: "Responsive service when you need help"

Everyone's right about what matters. But you can only have one Core Promise.

Why this happens:

Each department sees the business through their lens. Marketing sees differentiation. Sales sees close rates. Delivery sees feasibility. Support sees ticket volume. Without a forcing function, you'll try to be all things—which means you're nothing specific.

How to resolve it:

Step 1: Ask what you can deliver to EVERY customer, EVERY time.

- Marketing's "innovative solutions" - Can you innovate for every customer? No.
- Sales' "fast implementation" - Can you guarantee this for enterprise clients? Probably not.
- Delivery's "reliable software" - Can you deliver this consistently? Maybe.
- Support's "responsive service" - Can you respond consistently within a defined timeframe? Possibly.

This eliminates aspirations and focuses on operational reality.

Step 2: Test against your worst-case scenario.

Ask: "Can we deliver this promise on our worst day, with our worst-performing team member, for our most difficult customer?"

If no, it's not your Core Promise.

Step 3: Look at what you're already doing consistently.

Review the last 50 customer interactions. What did you actually deliver every single time? That pattern is your Core Promise, whether you've named it or not.

Step 4: Accept that some promises move to Supporting.

"Fast implementation" might be a Supporting Promise for certain customer tiers. "Responsive service" might be Supporting, not Core. The Core Promise is the foundation—everything else builds on it.

What success looks like: One sentence that everyone can recite. One promise that guides every decision. One commitment the entire company can deliver.

Challenge #2: Your Core Promise Feels Too Generic

What this looks like:

Your team settles on something like:

- "Quality products and excellent service"
- "Reliable solutions that meet customer needs"
- "Professional expertise delivered with care"

These sound like Core Promises. They're not. They're platitudes.

Why this happens:

You're trying to avoid excluding anyone. You're afraid specificity will limit your market. You want language that works for every customer segment, every use case, every future product.

The problem: Generic promises guide nothing. They can't be tested. They can't be broken (because they mean nothing). They can't drive decisions. You end up with words that sound professional but change nothing operationally.

How to resolve it:

Test 1: The Decision Test

Ask: "Would this Core Promise help us decide whether to build Feature X?"

If your answer is "maybe" or "it depends," your promise is too vague.

Example: "Quality products" doesn't tell you whether to add 50 new features or simplify to 10 core ones. "Simple software that requires no training" tells you exactly what to do.

Test 2: The Competitor Test

Ask: "Could our competitor claim this exact same Core Promise?"

If yes, it's too generic. Your Core Promise should reflect what's operationally true about YOU, not what's generally desirable in your industry.

Example: "Excellent customer service" - every company wants this. "Same-day response to support tickets" - this is specific to your operation.

Test 3: The Heroics Test

Ask: "Can we deliver this even when things go wrong?"

If your promise only works when everything's perfect, it's aspirational, not core.

Example: "Innovative solutions" - only works when R&D is hitting breakthroughs. "Reliable uptime above 99.5%" - can be delivered through systems and redundancy.

What to do: Add constraints. Add timeframes. Add scope. Turn "quality" into "durability tested to X standard." Turn "responsive" into "replies within 4 business hours." Turn "reliable" into "99.5% uptime with transparent status reporting."

Specificity feels limiting. That's the point. Limitations create clarity.

Challenge #3: You Realize You Can't Deliver Your Current Core Promise

What this looks like:

You go through the exercise and realize: "We've been promising 24-hour response times, but our average is 48 hours." Or: "We promise custom solutions, but 80% of clients get the same template." Or: "We claim to be the innovation leader, but we haven't shipped a major update in 18 months."

The gap between what you say and what you do is now undeniable.

Why this happens:

Your promise was set by marketing or sales without consulting delivery. Or it was true when you were smaller but doesn't scale. Or leadership committed to something aspirational, hoping the team would "figure it out."

Now you're faced with a choice: change your promise (and admit the gap) or change your operations (and invest heavily to close it).

How to resolve it:

Option A: Change Your Promise to Match Reality (Recommended for Most)

This feels like defeat. It's not. It's honesty.

Step 1: Acknowledge what you actually deliver consistently today.

If you respond in 48 hours, say 48 hours. If you deliver templated solutions with customization options, say that. If you ship incremental updates, not breakthroughs, own it.

Step 2: Reframe the promise around what you do well.

"48-hour response times with thorough resolution" is better than "24-hour response times" you miss constantly. "Proven solutions customized to your workflow" is better than "fully custom" when you're 80% templated.

Step 3: Update all promise-making channels in one coordinated push.

Don't let the old promise linger in legacy documentation, old marketing materials, or sales scripts. Kill it everywhere, all at once.

Step 4: Communicate the change transparently.

To customers: "We've updated our service commitment to reflect what we actually deliver consistently."

To the team: "We're aligning our promise with reality so we stop setting ourselves up to fail."

Option B: Change Your Operations to Match Your Promise (Expensive, Long Timeline)

Choose this path only if:

- The promise is central to your market position
- You have resources to invest (budget, time, talent)
- Leadership is committed for 12+ months
- You can survive the gap period while you close it

Step 1: Calculate what it would actually take.

Moving from 48-hour to 24-hour response might mean doubling support staff, adding weekend coverage, implementing new routing systems. Don't guess. Spec it fully.

Step 2: Build the capability before you re-promote the promise.

Don't promise 24-hour response until you've proven 30 consecutive days of delivery. Don't promise custom solutions until you've retooled your delivery process.

Step 3: Accept that you might need to narrow your market.

Keeping an ambitious promise often means saying no to customer segments you can't serve well. That's not failure—that's focus.

Option C: Do Nothing and Hope (Don't Do This)

Some companies choose to keep promising what they can't deliver, hoping no one notices or that they'll "figure it out eventually."

This is the path to customer churn, employee burnout, and reputational damage. The gap doesn't close itself. It widens.

What success looks like: Your promise and your delivery match. Your team isn't apologizing. Your customers aren't surprised. You've chosen honesty over aspiration—and your operations reflect it.

Challenge #4: Your Core Promise Changes Too Frequently

What this looks like:

Last quarter, your Core Promise was about speed. This quarter, it's about quality. Next quarter, leadership wants to focus on innovation. The promise shifts with strategy, with market trends, with whoever spoke to the CEO last.

Why this happens:

Leadership treats the Core Promise as a marketing message, not an operational commitment. Or the company is genuinely pivoting and hasn't stabilized. Or different executives have different visions and no one has forced alignment.

The problem: Your team can't operate effectively when the foundation keeps shifting. Systems built for speed contradict new focus on quality. Training for innovation contradicts push for reliability. Customers don't know what to expect from you.

How to resolve it:

Step 1: Distinguish between Core Promise and Strategic Priorities.

Your Core Promise should be stable for YEARS. It's the foundation.

Your strategic priorities can shift quarterly. They're the current focus.

Example:

- Core Promise (stable): "Reliable automation that works as configured"
- Q1 Priority: Speed up onboarding
- Q2 Priority: Expand enterprise features
- Q3 Priority: Improve mobile experience

The priorities change. The promise doesn't.

Step 2: Make changing your Core Promise a BIG DEAL.

It should require executive alignment, board discussion, company-wide communication. It shouldn't happen in a marketing meeting or a quarterly planning session.

Ask: "Are we fundamentally changing what we guarantee to every customer? Or are we just shifting where we invest?"

Usually, it's the latter. The Core Promise stays. The investments shift.

Step 3: Test whether it's really a Core Promise change.

Real Core Promise changes:

- Moving from "fast delivery" to "custom solutions" (fundamental operational shift)
- Moving from "lowest prices" to "highest quality" (complete business model change)
- Moving from "do-it-yourself platform" to "full-service solution" (target customer change)

NOT Core Promise changes:

- Adding new features
- Entering new markets
- Changing pricing tiers
- Launching new products

These expand your offering but don't change your foundational commitment.

What success looks like: Your Core Promise has been stable for 2+ years. Strategic priorities shift, but the foundation holds. Your team can build systems and processes knowing the promise won't change next quarter.

Challenge #5: Different Departments Operate With Different Core Promises

What this looks like:

Sales promises "same-day setup" while delivery promises "implementation within two weeks."

Marketing promises "customized to your business" while delivery delivers templatized solutions.

Support promises "always available" while actual hours are 9-5 weekdays.

Everyone has a Core Promise. None of them match.

Why this happens:

You never forced alignment. Or you defined a Core Promise but never trained the organization on it. Or each department optimized for their own metrics without considering the downstream impact.

How to resolve it:

Step 1: Surface the misalignment explicitly.

Run this exercise with cross-functional leadership:

- Have each department write down what they believe the Core Promise is
- Read them aloud
- Acknowledge the gaps without blame

The problem isn't that someone is wrong. The problem is that you're operating as separate companies.

Step 2: Choose ONE Core Promise that binds everyone.

Not "sales' promise" or "delivery's promise." THE company's promise.

This will require trade-offs:

- Sales might need to slow their pitch
- Marketing might need to be less aspirational
- Delivery might need to speed up or narrow scope
- Support might need to expand coverage

Every department gives something up so the company can deliver one consistent promise.

Step 3: Make it visible everywhere.

Put it on the wall in every office. Add it to email signatures. Reference it in every all-hands. Make it the first thing new hires learn.

Not because it's inspiring. Because it's operational truth.

Step 4: Hold departments accountable to it.

When sales promises something off-promise, call it out. When marketing creates content that contradicts it, send it back. When delivery suggests a process that breaks it, reject it.

The Core Promise is non-negotiable. Strategies change. Tactics change. The promise doesn't.

What success looks like: Ask any employee—from any department—what the Core Promise is. They all say the same thing. Not because they memorized it, but because they live it.

Worksheet: The Core Promise Builder

Step A: List your consistent outcomes (what do customers reliably get?)

Step B: List what customers depend on you for

Step C: Cross off anything that requires heroics

Step D: Cross off aspirations and marketing language

Step E: Draft 3 Core Promise options

Step F: Test each option

For each draft, ask:

- Does it reflect reality — not aspiration?
- Can your global Alignment Network deliver it without heroics?
- Would your delivery team, support team, and offshore team all say "yes, every time"?

Circle the one that passes all three checks.

Your Core Promise:

Next: In Chapter 2, you'll build your Promise Stack — the structured map of every promise your company makes, from the Core Promise down to the legacy promises still drifting through your systems.

TWO
THE PROMISE STACK

When AxisLine ran their first Drift Audit in Chapter 11, they were overwhelmed by what they found: 40+ Legacy Promises still living in outdated documentation, 12 Supporting Promises scattered across marketing materials, 8 Conditional Promises that sales was offering inconsistently, and 5 Experimental Promises that had leaked into production without anyone approving them.

Jasmine, leading their offshore support team, had been trying to keep promises the company made two product versions ago. Marketing was promoting features that delivery couldn't support. Sales was making custom commitments that no one had documented. The AI chatbot was guaranteeing response times no one had agreed to.

The problem wasn't that AxisLine made bad promises—it's that they had no system for organizing them. Every promise lived in isolation, with no clear hierarchy, no owner, and no expiration date. If your first Drift Audit feels like standing in front of a wall of sticky notes wondering how any of it happened — that's exactly where you're supposed to be. That discomfort is clarity arriving.

The Promise Stack solves this by organizing every promise your company makes into five clear layers. Here's how it works.

The Five Layers

Your Promise Stack has five distinct layers. Each serves a different purpose:

1. Core Promise — The one promise you keep every time

2. Supporting Promises — The promises that enable your Core Promise

3. Conditional Promises — Real promises, but only under specific conditions

4. Experimental Promises — Ideas, betas, prototypes not yet ready for customers

5. Legacy Promises — Promises that should have been buried but keep resurfacing

Here's what each layer means and how to use it.

1. Core Promise

This is your anchor. The one outcome your entire company rallies around. You defined this in Chapter 1.

Everything else in the Stack either supports it, conditions it, or distracts from it.

2. Supporting Promises

These are the operational commitments that *must* work for your Core Promise to be kept.

Examples:

- Predictable onboarding
- Accurate documentation
- Responsive support
- Timely delivery
- Consistent workflow performance

If a Supporting Promise breaks, your Core Promise breaks.

These are non-negotiable. They must be engineered into your operations, not hoped for.

3. Conditional Promises

This is where most companies fail. Conditional Promises are things you *can* do — but only when certain criteria are met.

Examples:

- Custom workflows (if data is clean)

- Expedited onboarding (if the customer is prepared)
- Advanced integrations (if systems are compatible)
- Same-day shipping (if products are in stock)
- Fast closings (if documents are verified early)

These are real promises. But they cannot be treated as guarantees.

The rule: Conditional Promises must be clearly labeled — internally and externally — or they create drift.

Mislabeling a Conditional Promise as a Supporting Promise is one of the fastest ways to destroy trust.

4. Experimental Promises

These are features, offerings, or capabilities that:

- Are being tested
- May change
- May not scale
- May never become real

Examples:

- Beta AI automation
- Early prototypes
- Pilot programs
- "In design" roadmap items

The rule: Experiments stay internal until they pass the Promise Gate.

Drift happens when Experimental Promises escape into the wild and customers believe they're real.

5. Legacy Promises

Legacy Promises are silent but dangerous.

They come from:

- Old marketing pages
- Outdated documentation
- Former sales scripts
- Sunset features
- Deprecated systems
- Past employee habits
- AI models trained on outdated data
- Cached online content

Legacy Promises continue influencing customer expectations long after they've stopped being true.

You *must* retire them — clearly, intentionally, and publicly when necessary.

How to Build Your Promise Stack

Step 1: Run the Drift Audit

When AxisLine ran their first Drift Audit in Chapter 11, they expected to find twenty or thirty promises. What covered the walls of their conference room was hundreds — surface promises, hidden promises, accidental promises, and legacy promises still circulating from campaigns years earlier. Most companies discover the same thing. The number is always larger than anyone expects.

Gather every promise your company might be making. Don't guess. Don't estimate. Actually collect them.

Sources to check:

- Website copy
- Sales scripts and decks
- Onboarding flows
- Support macros and knowledge base
- AI training datasets
- Old documentation

- Email sequences and automations
- Marketing content
- Product demos
- Partner collateral
- Internal Slack threads
- Offshore team scripts
- Customer assumptions (ask your support team what customers expect)

You're collecting raw truth — not opinions.

Step 2: Sort Each Promise Into a Layer

Use sticky notes, a whiteboard, or a digital tool. Your first pass will look messy. That's expected.

Then refine using these rules:

- **If you always deliver it** → Supporting or Core
- **If you sometimes deliver it** → Conditional
- **If it's not real yet** → Experimental
- **If it was real once but isn't anymore** → Legacy

Step 3: Validate With Your Alignment Network

Your delivery team, support team, offshore team, documentation owners, and AI governance team must validate each promise.

If they say, *"We can't deliver this every time"* — it moves down the stack.

This step is critical. Leadership teams often create stacks that sound right in the conference room but collapse in the field.

Step 4: Identify Promise Debt

Promise Debt = Promises that exceed your current capabilities.

These often live in Conditional, Experimental, or Legacy layers.

Each one creates misalignment, confusion, and cost. Flag them. You'll need to either retire them or invest in making them real.

AxisLine's Promise Debt was concentrated in their Legacy layer: 42 promises being retired — features that had been sunset, capabilities that had never scaled, and claims the AI chatbot was still making from training data built on old marketing copy. Naming the number made it real. Until then, the debt had been invisible.

Step 5: Confirm the Final Stack

Your final Promise Stack should be:

- Clean
- Precise
- Current
- Constrained to reality
- Understood by every team
- Governed by the Promise Gate
- The single source of truth for all communication

What Changes When You Have a Stack

Once your Promise Stack is clear:

- **Sales** knows exactly what they can and cannot promise.
- **Marketing** has boundaries for messaging.
- **Product** can prioritize what strengthens promises vs. what dilutes them.
- **Support** stops apologizing for mismatched expectations.
- **Offshore teams** stop guessing — they have a clear reference.
- **AI systems** can be trained to a single source of truth.
- **Leadership** makes faster decisions through one lens: Does this protect or dilute our promises?

The Promise Stack becomes the operating system for how your company speaks.

Industry Examples

Tech SaaS Platform:

- Core: We simplify complex workflows so they're immediately clear.
- Supporting: Clear onboarding, predictable uptime
- Conditional: Complex integrations
- Experimental: AI-driven workflow suggestions
- Legacy: "Unlimited customization"

Retail Brand:

- Core: Deliver quality products on time
- Supporting: Accurate inventory, reliable shipping
- Conditional: Same-day shipping
- Experimental: Virtual try-on
- Legacy: "Lifetime returns"

Real Estate:

- Core: Close transactions on schedule
- Supporting: Verified documents, transparent process
- Conditional: Fast-track closings
- Experimental: AI valuation tools
- Legacy: "We can close any deal"

Common Challenges When Building Your Promise Stack

Building your Promise Stack forces you to confront every promise your company has made—intentionally or accidentally. Here are the challenges that emerge and how to navigate them.

Challenge #1: You Have Too Many Promises to Organize

What this looks like:

Your Drift Audit revealed 80+ promises scattered across your website, marketing materials, sales decks, support docs, AI chatbot, and offshore team knowledge base. You're staring at a spreadsheet (or wall of sticky notes) feeling completely overwhelmed.

Where do you even start? How do you categorize 80 promises when you can barely remember making half of them?

Why this happens:

Companies accumulate promises over years without any system. Every new marketing campaign adds promises. Every sales conversation adjusts them. Every product update changes them. Every new team member interprets them differently. No one ever consolidated, categorized, or killed anything.

You're not dealing with 80 new promises. You're dealing with years of unmanaged accumulation.

How to resolve it:

Step 1: Start with the obvious Core Promise.

Don't try to organize all 80 at once. Start with the one promise that MUST be Core. You defined it in Chapter 1. Write it at the top of your Stack.

Everything else will organize around it.

Step 2: Sort the next tier: What directly supports Core?

Look through your list and ask: "Which promises are necessary to deliver the Core Promise?"

Example: If your Core Promise is "Reliable automation that works as configured," then "Uptime monitoring with transparent status" is probably Supporting. "Data backup and recovery" is probably Supporting. "Custom workflow builder" might be Supporting.

Don't overthink it. If it's essential to keeping your Core Promise, it's Supporting. Pull 8-12 promises into this layer.

Step 3: Identify obvious Legacy promises next.

These are easy to spot:

- Features you've deprecated
- Policies you've changed
- Pricing structures you've abandoned
- Services you no longer offer
- Guarantees you can't honor anymore

Pull these into a "Legacy" bucket. You'll decide what to do with them later. Just get them categorized.

Step 4: Look for Experimental promises.

Find anything that includes "beta," "pilot," "coming soon," "early access," or language like "we're testing" or "available to select customers." These are Experimental. Group them.

Step 5: Everything left is probably Conditional.

What remains likely includes:

- Promises tied to specific plans or tiers
- Services available only in certain regions
- Features that require add-ons or upgrades
- Custom capabilities for enterprise clients

If it's not Core, not Supporting, not Legacy, and not Experimental, it's probably Conditional.

Step 6: Accept that some will be hard to categorize.

You'll have 5-10 promises where you genuinely can't tell which layer they belong to. That's fine. Mark them as "TBD" and move on. As you fill in the obvious ones, these ambiguous promises will become clearer.

What success looks like: Your 80 promises are now in 5 buckets. Not perfectly organized, but categorized enough to work with. You've gone from chaos to structure in a few hours.

Challenge #2: You Can't Agree on Which Layer a Promise Belongs To

What this looks like:

Marketing thinks "24/7 support" is Core. Support knows it's Conditional (only for Enterprise tier). Sales has been telling prospects it's Supporting (available to everyone for an add-on fee). Product thought you deprecated it last year (Legacy).

You're looking at one promise and four different interpretations.

Why this happens:

Different departments see different aspects of the business. Marketing sees what differentiates you. Sales sees what closes deals. Support sees what they can actually deliver. Product sees what they built last quarter vs. this quarter.

No one is lying. They're just working with incomplete information.

How to resolve it:

Step 1: Ask: "Can we deliver this to EVERY customer?"

If yes → Could be Core or Supporting

If no → Definitely Conditional, Experimental, or Legacy

This eliminates ambiguity fast. "24/7 support" - Can you deliver it to every customer? If no, it's not Core or Supporting.

Step 2: Ask: "Is this necessary to deliver our Core Promise?"

If yes → It's Supporting

If no → It's Conditional, Experimental, or Legacy

"24/7 support" - Is this necessary to deliver "Reliable automation"? No. Automation works whether support is 24/7 or business hours. So it's not Supporting.

Step 3: Ask: "Who can actually access this?"

If everyone → Core or Supporting

If specific tiers/plans → Conditional

If pilot/beta group → Experimental

If nobody anymore → Legacy

"24/7 support" - Who can access it? Only Enterprise tier. Therefore: Conditional.

Step 4: Document the decision and the reasoning.

Don't just categorize. Write down WHY.

"24/7 support = Conditional (Enterprise only). Not Core because not all customers receive it. Not Supporting because it's not necessary to deliver Core Promise. Available as tiered service."

This prevents the same debate next quarter.

Step 5: Accept that some promises will move between layers.

A promise might be Experimental today (new beta feature) and Supporting next quarter (rolled out to everyone). Or Conditional today (Enterprise only) and deprecated next year (Legacy).

That's fine. The Stack is a living document. What matters is that everyone agrees on where it is RIGHT NOW.

What success looks like: When someone asks "What layer is Promise X?", your team can answer consistently. Not because they memorized it, but because the logic is documented and clear.

Challenge #3: Team Wants to Keep Legacy Promises That Should Die

What this looks like:

Your Drift Audit revealed a promise you made three years ago: "Free on-site training for all customers." You stopped offering this 18 months ago, but it's still on your website, in sales decks, and in offshore team scripts.

When you suggest moving it to Legacy and killing it, the team pushes back:

"But some customers still ask for it."

"What if we want to bring it back someday?"

"Can't we just keep it for enterprise clients?"

"This is what made us different from competitors."

No one wants to let it go.

Why this happens:

Legacy promises often represent what the company WANTED to be. They're aspirational. They're differentiated. They're what made you special when you were smaller or better resourced or had different priorities.

Killing them feels like admitting defeat. Like becoming generic. Like losing your soul.

But keeping them is worse. Every Legacy promise that lingers creates confusion, sets false expectations, and forces your team to apologize or scramble.

How to resolve it:

Step 1: Separate sentiment from operational reality.

Ask: "Do we currently deliver this promise?"

Not "Could we deliver it if we tried really hard?" Not "Did we deliver it once upon a time?" Not "Might we deliver it in the future?"

Do we deliver it TODAY, CONSISTENTLY, to the customers we're making this promise to?

If no, it's Legacy. Full stop.

Step 2: Acknowledge what made it valuable.

Don't dismiss the team's attachment. Say: "I understand why this mattered. It differentiated us. It showed we cared about customer success. It was part of our identity."

Then add: "And it's not sustainable anymore. Keeping it hurts us more than killing it."

Step 3: Show the cost of keeping it.

Legacy promises aren't free. They cost you:

- Customer disappointment when they discover you don't actually deliver it
- Sales time explaining why the website promise doesn't apply
- Support time apologizing for the disconnect
- Offshore team confusion about what to tell customers
- Your credibility when promises don't match reality

Make the cost visible. It's not just clutter. It's active harm.

Step 4: Create a sunset plan with a deadline.

Don't let Legacy promises linger indefinitely. Set a kill date.

"We're removing 'free on-site training' from all customer-facing materials by end of Q2. After that date, any reference to it is a mistake that should be reported and fixed."

Step 5: Offer a replacement if appropriate.

If the Legacy promise served a real need, replace it with something you CAN deliver consistently.

"Free on-site training" → "Comprehensive video training library + live Q&A sessions twice monthly"

"24/7 phone support" → "24/7 ticket submission with 4-hour response guarantee"

"Custom development for every client" → "Customizable templates with professional services for advanced needs"

You're not abandoning the intent. You're aligning the promise with reality.

Step 6: Let some die without replacement.

Not every Legacy promise needs a replacement. Some were bad ideas from the start. Some don't fit your business model anymore. Some were only valuable in a different market context.

It's okay to just say: "We no longer promise this. We never should have. We're correcting it now."

What success looks like: Legacy promises get killed in one coordinated sweep. Every customer-facing channel is updated simultaneously. The team stops defending promises you can't keep and starts focusing on promises you can.

Challenge #4: Your Stack Keeps Growing
(Everything Feels Core or Supporting)

What this looks like:

You started with 1 Core Promise and 8 Supporting Promises. But every time someone proposes adding a promise, the argument is: "This is essential. This supports our Core Promise. This should be Supporting layer."

Now you have 1 Core Promise and 23 Supporting Promises. Your Stack isn't organized—it's bloated.

Why this happens:

Teams confuse "important" with "Core/Supporting." They confuse "valuable" with "necessary to deliver the Core Promise." They confuse "competitive advantage" with "foundational."

Without discipline, everything migrates to the top two layers.

How to resolve it:

Step 1: Ruthlessly apply the "necessary" test.

Supporting Promises must be NECESSARY to deliver the Core Promise. Not helpful. Not valuable. Not nice to have. NECESSARY.

Ask: "If we removed this promise entirely, could we still deliver our Core Promise?"

If yes → It's not Supporting. Move it to Conditional.

Example:

Core Promise: "Reliable automation that works as configured"

Test these promises:

- "Uptime monitoring" - Necessary to ensure reliability? YES. Supporting.
- "Email notifications" - Necessary? NO. Nice to have, but automation works without it. Conditional.

- "Mobile app access" - Necessary? NO. Automation runs whether you view it on mobile or not. Conditional.
- "Dedicated account manager" - Necessary? NO. Automation works without human hand-holding. Conditional (likely Enterprise tier).

Be ruthless. If it's not necessary, it doesn't belong in Supporting.

Step 2: Set a Supporting Promise limit.

Force yourself to cap Supporting Promises at 8-12. If someone wants to add a new one, they must remove an existing one or re-categorize it as Conditional.

This creates healthy debate: "Is this REALLY more foundational than what we already have?"

Step 3: Remember: Conditional doesn't mean unimportant.

Teams resist moving promises to Conditional because it sounds like a demotion. It's not.

Conditional means: "This is valuable, but not universal. It's available to specific customers under specific circumstances."

That's not a weakness. That's a business model. Tiered offerings, regional variations, and upgrade options are how companies scale profitably.

Step 4: Review your Stack quarterly.

Promises that were Supporting when you were smaller might need to move to Conditional as you scale. Promises that were Experimental might become Supporting once they're proven.

The Stack should evolve. Set a quarterly review to ask: "Does this still belong here?"

What success looks like: Your Stack has clear hierarchy. Core is singular. Supporting is 8-12 promises maximum. Everything else is appropriately categorized as Conditional or Experimental. Your team understands that Conditional isn't lesser—it's different.

Challenge #5: Offshore or Distributed Teams Operate With a Different Stack

What this looks like:

Your headquarters team just spent three weeks building the Promise Stack. You're confident everyone is aligned. Then you talk to your offshore support team in Manila and discover:

They're still using promises from 18 months ago.

They have a completely different list of "what we guarantee."

They've never seen your new Stack.

They're being held accountable to promises you deprecated last quarter.

You don't have one Stack. You have multiple Stacks running in parallel.

Why this happens:

Distributed teams are the last to receive updates. Training happens slowly. Documentation gets translated or adapted and loses fidelity. Time zone differences make real-time alignment hard. Or teams were never brought into the Stack-building process in the first place.

How to resolve it:

Step 1: Include distributed teams in Stack creation from day one.

Don't build the Stack at headquarters and then "roll it out" to offshore teams. Bring them into the process.

Why? Because they're promise keepers. They know what customers ask for. They know what's actually deliverable. They know where current promises break. They have essential input.

If they weren't involved in building your Stack, rebuild it with their input. Yes, this takes time. Yes, it's worth it.

Step 2: Translate the Stack literally—don't adapt it.

When distributing the Stack to teams in other regions or languages, translate it word-for-word. Don't let regional teams "adapt it to local market."

Why? Because the whole point of the Stack is organizational alignment. "Local adaptation" = local drift.

The Core Promise is the same in Manila as it is in Austin. The Supporting Promises don't change based on time zone.

Step 3: Make the Stack the single source of truth.

Give distributed teams access to the live Stack document. Not a PDF from last quarter. Not a printed handout. The LIVE, version-controlled Stack.

When something changes, it changes everywhere simultaneously. No one operates on outdated information.

Step 4: Train offshore teams on how to USE the Stack.

Don't just send them the document. Train them:

- How to check if a promise is in the Stack before making it
- What to do when a customer asks for something not in the Stack
- Who to contact when they spot drift
- How to propose additions or changes

They need to know the Stack isn't just a reference document—it's operational policy.

Step 5: Create a feedback loop.

Distributed teams spot drift first. They hear customer confusion. They get asked for promises no one told them about. They see where documentation contradicts the Stack.

Create a channel for them to flag misalignment:

- Dedicated Slack channel
- Weekly Standup agenda item
- Drift reporting form

Make it easy to say: "I found a promise that's not in the Stack" or "Customer expects X but Stack says Y."

  THE PROMISE STACK

Step 6: Audit offshore-specific materials.

Your main website might be updated, but what about:

- Offshore team knowledge base articles
- Translated documentation
- Regional landing pages
- Chat scripts and templates
- Email response templates

These often contain legacy promises that headquarters forgot about. Audit them specifically and align them to the Stack.

What success looks like: Your offshore team in Manila can recite the Core Promise. They reference the Stack during customer conversations. When they spot drift, they report it immediately. They're not operating on outdated information—they're part of one aligned organization.

Worksheet: Promise Stack Mapping

A. List all discovered promises: (Continue collecting — most companies find 50-200+)

B. Categorize into layers:

Core Promise:

Supporting Promises:

Conditional Promises:

Experimental Promises:

Legacy Promises:

C. Identify inconsistencies: (Promises that appear in multiple places with different wording or conditions)

D. List promises to retire: (Legacy promises that must be eliminated)

E. List promises needing Gate review: (New or unclear promises that need validation)

Next: In Chapter 3, you'll install the Promise Gate — the checkpoint that prevents new promises from slipping through unchecked.

THREE
THE PROMISE GATE

Remember in Chapter 14 when Theo's sales team rebelled against the Gate? Half the team stormed out of the meeting. Theo was left sitting alone, convinced his team would mutiny. "They hate me," he told Marcus. "They think I'm making it impossible for them to do their jobs."

The Gate felt like bureaucracy. Like saying "no" to revenue. Like slowing down in a market that demanded speed.

It took three months before Theo's team saw the truth: The Gate wasn't slowing them down—it was protecting them. It stopped them from making promises they couldn't keep. It prevented angry customer calls. It eliminated the apologizing and scrambling that had become their daily routine. By Chapter 17, Theo's team wasn't just accepting the Gate—they were asking to add it to their CRM so they could check promises in real-time.

The Gate works. But only if you install it correctly and hold the line when people push back. Here's how to do both.

What the Promise Gate Does

The Promise Gate is a structured checkpoint that every new or changed promise must pass through before it reaches a customer.

Think of it as the customs checkpoint for every claim, feature, message, and expectation before it enters your business.

If it doesn't pass the Gate, it doesn't go public.

The Gate prevents:

- Improvisation
- Overpromising
- Legacy drift
- AI hallucinations

- Roadmap inflation
- Unclear messaging
- Internal misalignment

And it reinforces:

- Truth
- Clarity
- Accountability
- Consistency
- Brand credibility
- Operational health

The 3 Gate Questions

Every promise must pass all three of these questions:

1. CAN we do this?

Feasibility Check

Is this technically, operationally, or logistically possible *today*, without heroics?

If the answer is "maybe" → It fails.

2. SHOULD we do this?

Alignment Check

Does it reinforce our Core Promise and strengthen our Promise Stack?

If it pulls us into distraction or drift → It fails.

3. WILL we do this?

Commitment Check

Is the company prepared to deliver this promise *every time*, with consistency, clarity, and confidence?

If any part of your Alignment Network cannot support it → It fails.

What Goes Through the Gate

Anything that could become a promise — intentionally or unintentionally — must pass the Gate:

- **Marketing:** Landing pages, paid ads, email sequences, content pillars, brand claims
- **Sales:** Outbound messaging, demo language, proposal wording, feature commitments
- **Product:** Roadmap statements, feature availability, integration capabilities
- **Support:** Knowledge base articles, scripts, macros, automated responses
- **Offshore Teams:** Documentation, SOPs, customer handoff messages
- **AI & Automations:** Training datasets, chatbots, workflow triggers, autogenerated messaging
- **Leadership:** Investor updates, company announcements, strategic vision statements

Installing the Promise Gate

Step 1: Create a Central Intake Form

Build a simple form where teams submit anything that could create a customer expectation:

- New claims
- Feature requests
- Marketing ideas
- Product descriptions
- Customer commitments
- AI training prompts

- Demo scripts

This becomes the front door for all promises.

Step 2: Form a Cross-Functional Gate Committee

3-5 people representing:

- Delivery
- Support
- Sales
- Product
- Marketing
- AI / Ops
- Offshore (when possible)

Their job is to evaluate submissions honestly — not politically, not optimistically, not aspirationally. Realistically.

Step 3: Evaluate Using the 3 Gate Questions

For each submission, answer:

CAN we do this? → If not, reject or re-scope

SHOULD we do this? → If not, decline or delay

WILL we do this consistently? → If not, redesign or restructure

Step 4: Update the Promise Stack

If a promise passes the Gate:

- Add it to the Supporting or Conditional layer
- Update documentation
- Train Sales
- Update onboarding

- Train AI
- Update offshore scripts

If it fails, route it to:

- Experimental (if future potential)
- Legacy (if retired permanently)

Step 5: Publish the "Allowed Promises List"

This list becomes the single source of truth for:

- What Sales can promise
- What Marketing can say
- What Product can commit
- What Support can guarantee
- What AI can output

It reduces confusion by orders of magnitude.

Department-Specific Gatekeeping Rules

Sales Gatekeeping:

- No improvisation
- No "stretch" statements
- No roadmap promises
- No conditional promises without clearly stating conditions

Marketing Gatekeeping:

- No buzzwords that imply capabilities
- No resurrecting legacy claims
- No publishing unapproved language

Product Gatekeeping:

- No roadmap dates unless guaranteed
- No capability assumptions
- No "soft launches" leaking into public view

Support Gatekeeping:

- No macros written from memory
- No outdated knowledge base articles
- No improvising policies

Offshore Gatekeeping:

- No using old scripts
- No guessing when unclear
- No inherited phrasing from past eras

AI Gatekeeping:

- No training data outside the Stack
- No generative claims about features
- No legacy content allowed
- No unverified answers

Real Examples

Tech SaaS:

A salesperson promises "advanced automation."

Gate confirms: Only basic automation exists → Conditional. Advanced automation is experimental → cannot be promised.

Promise rejected.

Retail:

Marketing wants to advertise "same-day delivery."

Gate checks fulfillment: Only possible in 4 metro areas → Conditional.

Ad is rewritten: *"Same-day delivery available in select cities."*

Real Estate:

Agent wants to guarantee a fast closing.

Gate checks: Only fast if documents are verified early → Conditional.

Promise updated: *"Fast closing available for fully prepared clients."*

Common Challenges When Installing the Promise Gate

The Promise Gate is where theory meets reality. It forces trade-offs, slows enthusiasm, and creates friction. Here's how to navigate the pushback and challenges that inevitably emerge.

Challenge #1: Sales Team Rebels Against the Gate

What this looks like:

You announce the Promise Gate at the all-hands. Sales immediately pushes back:

"This will kill our close rates."

"Competitors don't have approval processes—we'll lose deals."

"You're tying our hands when we need to be nimble."

"We know what customers need. We don't need permission to sell."

Some salespeople ignore the Gate entirely. Others comply resentfully. A few threaten to quit.

Why this happens:

Sales is compensated on closing deals. The Gate feels like an obstacle between them and commission. They've been succeeding by saying "yes" quickly—now you're asking them to slow down and say "maybe, let me check."

They see the Gate as bureaucracy created by people who don't understand sales. They're not wrong that it creates friction. They're wrong that it's bad for the business.

How to resolve it:

Step 1: Acknowledge the legitimate concern.

Don't dismiss their fear. Say: "You're right that the Gate adds a step. You're right that it might slow some deals. I understand why this feels like we're making your job harder."

Then add: "And here's what we're protecting you from."

Step 2: Show them the cost of no Gate.

Pull recent examples where promises made in sales created problems downstream:

- Custom features promised that product couldn't deliver
- Timeline commitments delivery couldn't meet
- Service levels support couldn't sustain
- Pricing structures that lost money

Make it personal: "Remember the Johnson account? You promised same-day implementation. Delivery needed two weeks. The customer was furious. You spent three months managing their anger instead of closing new deals."

The Gate isn't creating problems. It's preventing them.

Step 3: Start with observation, not enforcement.

For the first 30 days, don't block anything through the Gate. Just observe.

Tell sales: "Run everything through the Gate. We'll approve everything while we calibrate. This is data collection, not enforcement."

Track:

- How many promises come through

                                            THE PROMISE GATE

- Which ones would have failed the Gate questions
- What happens to deals that involved off-Stack promises

After 30 days, show the data. Let sales see their own patterns.

Step 4: Make the Gate fast.

If Gate approval takes 48 hours, sales is right to be frustrated. Make the process:

- Under 2 hours for standard requests during business hours
- Clear escalation path for urgent deals
- Simple form (3 questions, not 20 fields)

Speed reduces resistance. The Gate should clarify, not strangle.

Step 5: Show them early wins.

When the Gate prevents a disaster, celebrate it publicly:

"The Gate caught a promise for 24/7 support on the Standard tier. If we'd said yes, we'd be scrambling to staff nights and weekends or apologizing to the customer in two weeks. Gate saved us."

Sales needs to see the Gate working FOR them, not against them.

Step 6: Give sales approved promise options.

Don't make them invent promises from scratch. Give them a menu:

- "Here are pre-approved promises you can make to any customer"
- "Here are Conditional promises you can make to Enterprise tier"
- "Here are promises that need Gate approval before offering"

This removes guesswork and speeds conversations.

What success looks like: Three months after Gate installation, sales uses it proactively. They check before promising instead of apologizing after. They see it as protecting their reputation, not blocking their success.

What this looks like:

Before the Gate: Sales promised features, marketing launched campaigns, product announced roadmaps, support made guarantees. Fast. Autonomous. No approval needed.

After the Gate: Everything stops. Every promise needs review. The Gate Committee meets once a week. Requests pile up. Deals wait. Momentum dies.

Your team says: "We've gone from nimble startup to corporate bureaucracy. The Gate is killing our speed."

Why this happens:

You designed the Gate as a safeguard but didn't design it for throughput. You created a review process without considering volume. You made the committee the bottleneck.

The Gate isn't inherently slow. Your Gate PROCESS is slow.

How to resolve it:

Step 1: Separate routine from exception.

Most promises don't need committee review. They need triage:

Tier 1: Pre-approved (no Gate needed)

Promises already in your Stack. Sales can make these anytime. Marketing can use these freely. No approval required.

Tier 2: Minor modifications (fast Gate)

Small adjustments to existing promises. Example: Customer wants "4-hour response" instead of standard "same-day." One Gate member can approve via Slack in 15 minutes.

Tier 3: New promises (full Gate review)

Brand new commitments. These go to committee. But this should be 5-10% of total volume, not 100%.

Triage ruthlessly. Only exception cases go to committee.

Step 2: Empower Gate members to approve individually for low-risk promises.

Don't require full committee for everything. Give each Gate member authority to approve:

- Promises under $X value
- Promises within established parameters
- Time-bound pilot commitments

Save committee time for genuinely complex decisions.

Step 3: Set response time SLAs for the Gate itself.

Make the Gate accountable:

- Tier 1 (pre-approved): Instant
- Tier 2 (minor modification): 2 hours during business hours
- Tier 3 (new promise): 24 hours maximum

If the Gate misses its SLA, escalate. The Gate should clarify quickly, not delay indefinitely.

Step 4: Create an urgent bypass process (with accountability).

Sometimes deals genuinely can't wait 24 hours. Create a bypass:

"For deal-critical urgency, you can bypass the Gate with two conditions:

1. You get verbal approval from your department head
2. You submit the promise for Gate review within 24 hours post-close"

This keeps deals moving while maintaining accountability. Bypass should be rare (under 5% of promises). If it's happening constantly, your Tier 1/2 categories are too narrow.

Step 5: Batch review routine requests.

Don't review promises one-by-one as they arrive. Batch them:

- 10am daily Gate review (Tier 2 requests)
- Weekly committee (Tier 3 requests)

Batching is more efficient than context-switching all day.

What success looks like: 90% of promises get handled in Tier 1 (instant) or Tier 2 (within 2 hours). Only genuinely new or complex promises go to committee. The Gate clarifies without strangling. Speed is maintained.

Challenge #3: How to Handle "But the Customer Needs This NOW" Requests

What this looks like:

Sales is on the phone with a prospect. The deal is $250K. The prospect asks: "Can you provide weekly executive briefings?" It's not in your Stack. It's not pre-approved. But the sale might depend on saying yes right now.

Sales comes to you: "We need Gate approval in the next 30 minutes or we lose the deal. Can we bypass just this once?"

This happens weekly. The Gate is constantly under pressure to approve "just this once" exceptions.

Why this happens:

Real business has urgency. Prospects don't wait 24 hours for Gate approval. Competitors say yes immediately. Your process wasn't designed for deal-time pressure.

If you say no, you might lose revenue. If you say yes, the Gate becomes meaningless.

How to resolve it:

Step 1: Distinguish between urgency and importance.

Ask: "Is this urgent because the customer needs it now, or urgent because we failed to anticipate it?"

If it's a common request you should have anticipated → Add it to pre-approved list for future. But this instance still goes through Gate process.

If it's genuinely unique → Might warrant fast-track.

Step 2: Create a 60-minute fast-track Gate.

For deal-critical moments:

- Sales submits Gate request via dedicated Slack channel
- Tags it "URGENT - active deal"
- Provides deal value, customer name, specific promise requested
- Gate member responds within 60 minutes (during business hours)

Decision is: approve, deny, or approve-with-modifications.

60 minutes is fast enough for most deals, slow enough for thoughtful review.

Step 3: Apply the three Gate questions ruthlessly, even under pressure.

Don't skip the questions because it's urgent:

1. **CAN we deliver this?** Do we have capability?
2. **SHOULD we deliver this?** Does it align with Core Promise?
3. **WILL we deliver this?** Do we have resources/commitment?

If any answer is "no" or "unclear," the answer is no. Urgency doesn't change capability or alignment.

Step 4: Offer approved alternatives in real-time.

When you can't approve the specific request, don't just say no. Offer alternatives:

"We can't do weekly executive briefings (not in our model), but we CAN do monthly business reviews plus ad-hoc executive calls as needed. Would that work?"

Sales can pivot in real-time instead of losing the deal.

Step 5: Track "lost deals due to Gate" honestly.

Don't assume every "no" costs you the deal. Track:

- How many deals requested off-Stack promises
- How many we declined
- How many we actually lost

Often, you'll find that saying no didn't kill the deal. The customer accepted the alternative, or the promise wasn't actually a dealbreaker, or they bought anyway.

If you're genuinely losing significant revenue due to Gate restrictions, that's data to revisit your Stack—not bypass the Gate.

What success looks like: Urgent requests get 60-minute turnaround. Sales knows how to get fast Gate approval when needed. But "urgent" is reserved for real urgency, not routine requests.

⸺

Challenge #4: Different Departments Interpret Gate Decisions Differently

What this looks like:

The Gate approved "priority support" for Enterprise tier. But what does "priority" mean?

Sales thinks it means: "Dedicated account manager responds within 1 hour"

Support thinks it means: "Tickets get looked at first, but still within our 24-hour SLA"

Product thinks it means: "Feature requests get prioritized in roadmap"

Same Gate decision. Three different interpretations. Three different promises being made.

Why this happens:

The Gate approved the concept but didn't define the specifics. Everyone filled in the blanks based on their department's perspective.

This is how drift starts AFTER the Gate. You prevented one problem but created another.

How to resolve it:

Step 1: Gate approvals must include specific definitions.

Don't approve vague concepts. Approve specific, operational promises.

Bad Gate approval: "Yes, we can offer priority support to Enterprise"

Good Gate approval: "Yes, we can offer priority support defined as: Tickets tagged and reviewed within 2 hours during business hours (9am-6pm ET Mon-Fri). Response SLA: 4 hours. Resolution target: 24 hours. No dedicated account manager. No roadmap prioritization."

The Gate decision should be implementable without interpretation.

Step 2: Require Gate decisions to specify:

- Exactly what's promised (the specific commitment)
- Who delivers it (which team/department)
- When it applies (conditions, tiers, timeframes)
- What it doesn't include (explicit exclusions)

If the Gate request doesn't include these details, send it back for clarification before approving.

Step 3: Publish approved promises immediately.

When the Gate approves something, update the Stack within 24 hours. Don't let approved promises live in email threads or Slack conversations.

Add it to the official Stack document with the full definition. Make it visible to everyone.

Step 4: Require cross-functional review for new promise categories.

If the Gate is approving a promise that will affect multiple departments (like "priority support"), require representatives from each affected department to review the definition BEFORE approval.

Sales, support, and product should all see and agree to the specific definition. This prevents interpretation drift.

Step 5: Create a Gate decision log.

Maintain a running record of:

- What was requested
- What was approved/denied
- The specific definition
- Date and rationale

This creates an audit trail and prevents re-litigating the same decisions later.

What success looks like: When the Gate approves "priority support," everyone—sales, support, product, offshore teams—describes it identically. The definition is documented, published, and unambiguous.

Challenge #5: The Gate Becomes a Rubber Stamp (Approves Everything)

What this looks like:

You installed the Gate six months ago. Initially, it rejected or modified 30% of requests. Now it approves 95% of everything.

The Gate has become a formality. Sales submits requests knowing they'll be approved. The committee doesn't push back. The three Gate questions are asked but not really debated.

The Gate exists, but it's not protecting you anymore.

Why this happens:

Gate fatigue. The committee got tired of being the "department of no." They faced pressure from leadership to "not block revenue." They approved a few questionable promises and nothing broke immediately, so they got looser with standards.

Or the opposite: the team got so good at self-screening that only obviously-approvable promises reach the Gate. But you can't tell the difference between "high-quality submissions" and "rubber stamp drift."

How to resolve it:

Step 1: Audit recent Gate approvals.

Pull the last 50 Gate decisions. For each approval, re-ask the three questions honestly:

1. CAN we deliver this? (Do we have capability?)
2. SHOULD we deliver this? (Does it align with Core Promise?)
3. WILL we deliver this? (Do we have resources committed?)

If you find approvals where the honest answer to any question is "no" or "unclear," your Gate has drifted.

Step 2: Track promises-made vs. promises-kept.

The ultimate test: Are we delivering what the Gate approved?

If the Gate approved "4-hour response times" but actual average is 8 hours, the Gate failed. It approved something we can't deliver.

Track this monthly. When Gate approvals aren't being kept, tighten standards.

Step 3: Rotate Gate committee members.

Gate fatigue is real. Bring in fresh perspectives every 6 months. New members ask harder questions. They haven't been worn down by months of pressure.

Keep one experienced member for continuity, rotate the other 2-3 positions.

Step 4: Make denial rate visible.

Track and publish: "This month the Gate approved 87%, denied 8%, modified 5%."

If approval rate approaches 95%+, ask: "Are we being rigorous enough, or is the team self-screening effectively?"

Investigate. Interview submitters. "Why did you submit this request? Did you think it might be denied?"

If they say "I knew it would be approved, the Gate always says yes," you have rubber stamp drift.

Step 5: Celebrate Gate denials as wins.

When the Gate says no and prevents a problem, make it visible:

"The Gate denied a request for custom integration that would have required 3 months of dev time we don't have. Saved us from over-promising."

Denials aren't failures. They're the Gate working correctly.

Step 6: Do a quarterly "what did we almost approve?" review.

Once per quarter, look at close calls—promises the Gate almost approved but had concerns about.

Ask: "If we'd said yes, what would have happened?"

This helps calibrate standards. Sometimes you'll find you were too cautious. Sometimes you'll find you almost made a mistake.

What success looks like: The Gate maintains rigor. Approval rate stays in the 75-85% range (high enough that submission is worth it, low enough that scrutiny is real). Denials are celebrated as drift prevention, not departmental friction.

Worksheet: Promise Gate Setup

A. Gate Committee Members:

B. Intake Form Location:

C. Gate Cadence:

□ Weekly □ Biweekly □ Continuous □ Other: __________

D. Submission Rules:

(Who can submit? What format? What detail is required?)

E. Approval Protocol:

(Who makes final decisions? How are ties broken?)

F. Communication Plan:

(How are Gate decisions communicated to teams?)

Next: In Chapter 4, you'll build the Alignment Rhythm — the cadence that keeps drift from returning.

FOUR

THE ALIGNMENT RHYTHM

There's a moment in every implementation when the consultant leaves. Victor walked out of AxisLine's office on a Friday afternoon, and by the following Tuesday — when the team ran their first Weekly Promise Standup without him — the system was already wobbling.

Nobody knew who was supposed to start. Tessa kept looking at the door. The meeting ran 90 minutes and resolved nothing. When it ended, Devon said what everyone was thinking: *"That was bad."*

It was. And it was also the most important meeting they ever ran — because they ran it. Not Victor. Them.

Six weeks later, that same team caught a Conditional Promise slipping into a marketing email before it reached a single customer. Week eight, the offshore team flagged a LinkedIn ad containing unapproved language and killed it within the hour.

That progression, from chaos to catch, is what the Alignment Rhythm builds. Not by making the first standup perfect. By making sure there *is* a next standup.

The Four Pillars of Rhythm

PAS defines four rhythms that work together:

1. **Weekly Promise Standup** — Catch drift early
2. **Monthly Stack Review** — Keep the system current
3. **Quarterly Gate Calibration** — Adapt to reality
4. **Annual Promise Reset** — Ensure promises match who you've become

Together, they keep your company aligned across people, systems, departments, global teams, and AI.

1. Weekly Promise Standup

Purpose: Catch drift before it escalates

Duration: 10-15 minutes; max 30 minutes

Attendees:

- Sales lead
- Marketing lead
- Product lead
- Delivery
- Support
- Offshore representative
- AI governance or ops (if applicable)

Agenda:

A. Wins (2 minutes)

Where did alignment work this week?

- A salesperson used the Gate
- A knowledge base got corrected
- Offshore flagged drift
- AI models stayed aligned
- Delivery hit expectations with ease

This reinforces positive behavior.

B. Drift Sightings (5 minutes)

Where did alignment slip?

- A rep promised something too early
- A landing page used outdated language
- A new product concept leaked
- Customers referenced old claims
- Chatbots hallucinated old capabilities

Drift sightings should be celebrated, not punished. Spotting drift is a sign of alignment maturity.

C. Gate Decisions (3 minutes)

Anything that needs Gate review is noted and scheduled.

D. Actions (5 minutes)

Each drift item gets an owner and next step.

Why Weekly Matters:

Weekly keeps drift from becoming customer frustration, support tickets, brand erosion, product confusion, or lost revenue.

Weekly = early detection.

In Week 5 of AxisLine's Rhythm, the team ran their first Monthly Stack Review that actually worked. They found four new Conditional Promises needing clarification, two Legacy Promises still floating in the system, and three Experimental features that had leaked into demo decks — and fixed every one of them in a single meeting. That's early detection turning into same-day correction.

2. Monthly Stack Review

Purpose: Ensure your Promise Stack stays accurate and relevant

Duration: 60 minutes

Attendees: Department heads + Alignment Network representatives

Agenda:

A. Review Supporting Promises

Are we consistently meeting them? If not — why?

B. Update Conditional Promises

Have conditions changed? Do customers understand them?

C. Review Experimental Promises

Are any ready to move up the stack? Should any be retired?

D. Identify New Legacy Promises

What drifted in the past month that's now outdated?

- An integration we sunset
- A feature we redesigned
- A shipping method discontinued
- A marketing claim no longer accurate

E. Validate the Core Promise

Is it still true? Still deliverable? Still differentiating?

The Core Promise rarely changes, but validating it monthly builds discipline.

F. Update Documentation & AI Training

Any Stack changes must cascade into:

- AI models
- Scripts
- Knowledge bases
- Internal docs
- Sales tools
- Onboarding materials

This prevents old truth from resurrecting itself.

Why Monthly Matters:

This meeting ensures your Stack evolves intentionally — not reactively.

Without monthly oversight, Conditional Promises sneak upward, Experimental Promises leak outward, and Legacy Promises reappear silently.

Monthly = system integrity.

AxisLine's Week 8 is the clearest proof of monthly oversight working. Maria from Manila pinged the leadership channel: three customers that day had asked about "hyper-flex automation." It wasn't in the Stack. Rina searched, found it in a LinkedIn ad that hadn't been updated, and killed it within the hour. One message. One search. One hour. That's what a functioning Rhythm makes possible.

3. Quarterly Gate Calibration

Purpose: Ensure your Promise Gate stays strong as your business evolves

Duration: 90 minutes

Attendees: Gate Committee + leadership + PAS Advisor

Your PAS Advisor is an external partner who has worked with your Promise Stack and Gate from the outside. Someone who can see the promise drift your internal teams have become too close to notice. At AxisLine, Victor returned quarterly specifically for this meeting. His value wasn't in the agenda; it was in the questions he asked that no one inside the room thought to ask.

Find yours at promisealignment.com.

Agenda:

A. Gate Performance Review

- How many promises entered the company?
- How many passed?
- How many should not have passed?
- Which departments struggled?
- Did any unapproved promises leak out?

B. Checklist Update

Refine checklists for:

- Sales commitments
- Marketing claims

- Product roadmap wording
- Support guarantees
- AI training rules
- Offshore scripts

C. Criteria Recalibration

The Gate must evolve with capabilities. Ask:

- Can we now handle certain Conditional Promises consistently?
- Are some Supporting Promises unrealistic and need redesign?
- Are new Experimental Promises gaining traction?

D. Alignment Network Feedback

Your delivery teams tell the truth about what really happens. Their feedback sharpens the Gate.

Why Quarterly Matters:

Capabilities evolve. Markets shift. Teams grow. AI improves. Documentation expands.

Calibration keeps the Gate realistic, strong, and credible.

Quarterly = sustainable alignment.

At AxisLine's first Quarterly Review in the Epilogue, the team surfaced two failures that the weekly Standups had missed: a Conditional Promise that had slipped into marketing copy without Gate review, and a new product manager who had tried to add features without Stack approval. Neither failure was catastrophic. Both were correctable. The quarterly review is what made them visible before they compounded.

4. Annual Promise Reset

Purpose: Ensure your promises still match the company you've become

Duration: 2 day strategic session

Attendees: Full leadership team + key Alignment Network representatives + PAS Advisor

The Annual Promise Reset is where the PAS Advisor's outside perspective carries the most weight. This is the session where companies are most tempted to rationalize drift rather than fix it — to call a Legacy Promise "still relevant," to move an Experimental Promise into Supporting before it's ready, to avoid the hard conversation about whether the Core Promise still fits. An external advisor has no stake in those rationalizations. Victor's role at Axis-Line's Annual Session wasn't to run the meeting — it was to ask the question no one else would: "Is this still true?"

This is the strategic annual ritual where leaders:

- Revisit the Core Promise
- Clean the Stack
- Retire outdated promises
- Redefine Conditional and Supporting layers
- Redesign documentation
- Update AI truth sources
- Modernize the Alignment Network
- Remove legacy claims
- Unify global teams
- Ensure the entire brand reflects reality

This is not a rebrand. It's a reality refresh.

Agenda:

A. Is our Core Promise still true?

If not — redefine it.

B. Do Supporting Promises still reflect consistent delivery?

If not → elevate capabilities or reduce promises.

C. Which Conditional Promises should become Supporting?

This is a strong indicator of growth.

　　　　　　　　　　　THE ALIGNMENT RHYTHM

D. Which Experimental Promises failed?

Retire them. Free up energy.

E. Which Legacy Promises must be eliminated?

This keeps your identity clean.

F. Update the public-facing brand

Website, materials, AI — all must match the updated truth.

G. Alignment Network Re-Training

Everyone gets re-aligned to the new reality.

Why Annual Matters:

Companies evolve. Promises must evolve with them. Annual alignment ensures your business remains clear, competitive, and trusted.

Annual = long-term durability.

Why the Rhythm Works

The Alignment Rhythm makes alignment a habit — not a rescue mission.

It prevents drift from compounding. It reinforces the truth your company is built on. Over time, it makes alignment feel less like discipline and more like identity.

And it reinforces truth, clarity, consistency, operational discipline, customer trust, global cohesion, and cultural strength.

The Alignment Rhythm is the heartbeat of PAS.

Each part supports the others. Each part reinforces the Promise Stack, the Core Promise, and the Gate. This is how companies sustain alignment long-term.

The Alignment Rhythm—Weekly Standups, Monthly Stack Reviews, Quarterly Gate Calibration, and Annual Promise Resets—looks simple on paper. In practice, it's where discipline either takes root or dies. Here's how to navigate the challenges.

Challenge #1: Weekly Promise Standups Feel Like "Just Another Meeting"

What this looks like:

You launch Weekly Promise Standups. The first one goes okay. By week three, people show up late. By week five, half the team is multitasking. By week eight, someone asks: "Do we really need to keep doing this? We're all busy. Nothing's drifting."

Attendance drops. Participation becomes passive. The Standup becomes a formality people tolerate rather than value.

Why this happens:

Your team is drowning in meetings. They don't see immediate value from the Standup. It feels like reporting status they could share in Slack. The format is boring. No decisions get made. Nothing changes.

Without visible impact, the Standup dies from meeting fatigue.

How to resolve it:

Step 1: Keep it to 15 minutes. Ruthlessly.

The moment your Standup runs 30-45 minutes, you've lost. People zone out. It becomes a time sink.

Set a timer. When 15 minutes hits, stop—even mid-update. Anything unresolved goes to Slack or a separate working session.

Brevity creates urgency. People pay attention because they know it'll be over quickly.

Step 2: Use a strict format that prevents rambling.

Each person answers three questions ONLY:

1. **What promise drift did I spot this week?** (specific examples, not "everything's fine")
2. **What promise-related decision do I need help with?** (actual decisions, not updates)
3. **What's one thing we should add to the Stack, Gate, or kill from Legacy?** (actionable suggestion)

No project updates. No general status. No "just wanted to mention." If it's not about promises, it doesn't belong in this meeting.

Step 3: Make drift findings visible and celebrated.

When someone spots drift, celebrate it:

"Paolo flagged that our chatbot is promising same-day shipping on backorders. Great catch. We're fixing it today."

Don't let drift reports disappear into a void. Show that finding drift = preventing customer disappointment = success.

Keep a running tally: "This month we caught 12 instances of drift before they reached customers." Make the Standup's value measurable.

Step 4: Make decisions in the Standup, not later.

Don't defer everything to "we'll discuss offline." Small decisions should happen live:

"Should we add '4-hour response time' to Supporting Promises?" → Decide now. Yes or no. Two minutes of discussion maximum.

"Should we kill 'free on-site training' from Legacy?" → Decide now.

If decisions get made, the meeting has value. If everything is "we'll think about it," the meeting is waste.

Step 5: Rotate who runs the Standup.

Don't let one person (especially a leader) run it every week. Rotate facilitators across departments.

When marketing runs it one week, sales the next, delivery the next, everyone takes ownership. It's not "the boss's meeting"—it's the team's practice.

Step 6: Cancel it if nothing to discuss (occasionally).

If there's genuinely no drift to report, no decisions needed, and no Stack changes, cancel the Standup that week.

This prevents the Standup from becoming performative. "We're meeting because it's Tuesday" is how meetings die. "We're meeting because there's promise work to do" is how they stay valuable.

But don't cancel often. The rhythm matters. Most weeks should have something.

What success looks like: The Standup runs 12-15 minutes. People show up on time because they know it won't waste their time. Drift gets caught and fixed in real-time. Decisions get made. The meeting has energy, not obligation.

<hr>

Challenge #2: Monthly Stack Reviews Reveal Nothing (Or Everything)

What this looks like:

Scenario A: Reveals Nothing

You gather for Monthly Stack Review. Everyone reports: "No changes to the Stack. Everything's aligned. Nothing to update." The meeting ends in 10 minutes. You wonder if you're wasting time.

Scenario B: Reveals Everything

You gather for Monthly Stack Review. Everyone has changes: "Marketing added 6 new promises. Sales modified 4. Product deprecated 3. Support found 8 legacy promises." You spend 3 hours debating every change. Nothing gets resolved. Everyone leaves exhausted.

Both extremes are problems.

Why this happens:

Scenario A: Your team doesn't understand what a Stack Review is for. They think it's only for major changes. Or they're not actually checking their areas. Or they're afraid to report drift.

Scenario B: You have no governance. Everyone's making changes without coordination. The Monthly Review becomes the first time anyone sees what others have done. It's chaos.

How to resolve it:

For Scenario A (Nothing to Report):

Step 1: Assign specific Stack ownership.

Don't ask "anyone notice changes?" Ask specific people:

- Marketing: "Any new promises in campaigns launched this month?"
- Sales: "Any custom commitments made that aren't in the Stack?"
- Product: "Any features shipped or deprecated?"
- Support: "Any promises customers asked about that we couldn't find in the Stack?"
- AI/Systems: "Any new automated responses added?"

Direct accountability produces findings.

Step 2: Review specific channels, not general memory.

Don't rely on people remembering. Actually review:

- This month's marketing emails (scan for promises)
- Sales proposals closed this month (check for custom terms)
- Product release notes (look for capability promises)
- Top 10 support tickets (check for expectation gaps)

Stack Reviews should include actual artifact review, not just conversation.

Step 3: Ask: "What SHOULD be in the Stack but isn't?"

Sometimes the issue isn't that nothing changed—it's that you never documented promises you've been making all along.

"We've been offering implementation support to Enterprise clients for six months, but it's not in the Stack. Should we formalize it?"

Findings aren't just changes. They're gaps.

For Scenario B (Too Much to Process):

Step 1: Require pre-submission of Stack changes.

Don't show up to Monthly Review with surprises. Require:

- All proposed Stack changes submitted 48 hours before the meeting
- Changes include: what's being added/modified/removed, why, and which layer
- Gate approval already secured for new promises

The Monthly Review discusses pre-submitted changes, not discovers them for the first time.

Step 2: Batch similar changes.

If marketing added 6 new Supporting Promises, don't debate each one individually. Group them:

"Marketing added 6 Supporting Promises related to enterprise features. Here's the list. Any objections to adding all 6?"

If no objections, approve as a batch in 2 minutes.

Deep discussion only for controversial or unclear changes.

Step 3: Set a time limit per change.

Each Stack change gets 5 minutes maximum. If you can't resolve it in 5 minutes, defer to a working session outside the Review.

The Monthly Review approves clear changes and identifies complex ones that need deeper work.

What success looks like: Monthly Stack Reviews consistently take 45-60 minutes. You find 3-8 changes per month (enough to matter, not so many it's chaos). Changes are pre-submitted and discussed efficiently. The Stack stays current without endless debate.

<hr>

Challenge #3: Quarterly Gate Calibration Never Happens (Or Gets Skipped)

What this looks like:

You schedule Quarterly Gate Calibration for the first week of Q2. The meeting gets postponed because leadership is traveling. Rescheduled for week 3. Postponed again for budget planning. By week 8 of Q2, someone says: "Should we just skip it this quarter and do it next quarter?"

Quarterly Gate Calibration becomes the meeting that never happens.

Why this happens:

It's the least urgent of the four Rhythm pillars. Weekly Standups are habitual. Monthly Stack Reviews feel operational. Annual Promise Resets are big events. But Quarterly Gate Calibration feels optional.

Until the Gate drifts and you don't notice.

How to resolve it:

Step 1: Tie it to existing quarterly planning.

Don't make Gate Calibration a separate meeting. Embed it in quarterly business reviews or planning sessions that already happen.

"After we review Q1 results and set Q2 goals, we're spending 60 minutes calibrating the Gate."

Piggyback on existing rhythm instead of creating new calendar burden.

Step 2: Make the agenda concrete and valuable.

Gate Calibration shouldn't be vague "let's discuss the Gate." It should answer specific questions:

- **What did the Gate approve this quarter?** (review the log)
- **What did we deliver vs. what we approved?** (promises kept vs. broken)
- **Did we approve things we shouldn't have?** (drift detection)
- **Did we deny things we should have approved?** (too cautious?)
- **What patterns are we seeing in Gate requests?** (trends)

With this agenda, the meeting produces insights, not just discussion.

Step 3: Require cross-functional attendance.

If only one department shows up, it's not calibration—it's a department meeting.

Require representatives from:

- Sales (promise makers)
- Delivery (promise keepers)
- Support (drift detectors)
- Product (capability definers)

Their presence makes calibration meaningful. They see each other's perspectives on what the Gate approved and whether it was right.

Step 4: Use Gate Calibration to update Gate rules.

Don't just review past decisions. Improve future ones.

Ask: "What Gate question should we add based on this quarter's patterns?"

Example: "We approved 4 promises this quarter that required offshore team training we didn't budget for. New Gate question: 'Does this promise require new training for any team?'"

Gate Calibration should make the Gate smarter, not just audit it.

 THE ALIGNMENT RHYTHM

Step 5: Block the date 6 months in advance.

At the start of the year, block all 4 Quarterly Gate Calibration dates on leadership calendars. Non-negotiable. Treat it like board meetings or investor updates.

If it's on the calendar 6 months ahead, it's less likely to get bumped.

What success looks like: Quarterly Gate Calibration happens every quarter, on time, with full cross-functional attendance. The Gate gets measurably smarter each quarter. You catch calibration drift (too loose or too cautious) before it compounds.

Challenge #4: Annual Promise Reset Feels Too Big to Schedule

What this looks like:

Annual Promise Reset is supposed to be a 1-2 day strategic session where you fundamentally review your Core Promise, reassess your Stack, and realign the organization for the coming year.

But you can't get 1-2 days of leadership time. The calendars don't align. It gets pushed from January to March. Then someone suggests "let's just do it next year when we're less busy."

The Annual Reset becomes the thing you always plan to do but never actually schedule.

Why this happens:

Two full days feels impossible. Leadership can't clear their calendars. It seems too big, too theoretical, too much like a retreat.

But without the Annual Reset, your Core Promise slowly drifts from operational reality. Your Stack accumulates cruft. Alignment decays over 12 months.

How to resolve it:

Step 1: Start with a half-day, not two days.

Don't let "perfect" kill "good enough." If you can't get two days, start with 4 hours.

A focused half-day Annual Reset beats no Reset at all.

Half-day agenda:

- Hour 1: Review Core Promise (does it still reflect reality?)
- Hour 2: Review Stack layers (what should move or die?)
- Hour 3: Review Gate effectiveness (approve/deny rates, patterns)
- Hour 4: Set promise priorities for next year

This doesn't replace a full Reset long-term, but it prevents a year without any strategic promise review.

Step 2: Schedule it 12 months in advance.

At this year's Annual Reset, schedule next year's date before anyone leaves the room.

"Next year's Annual Promise Reset: January 15-16, 2027. Block your calendars now."

Leadership is more likely to protect time they blocked a year ago than time scheduled 3 weeks out.

Step 3: Make it off-site if possible.

Getting out of the office removes interruptions. People can't "just pop into the Reset for 20 minutes" if it's off-site.

Doesn't need to be expensive. A rented conference room across town works. The point is environmental separation from daily operations.

Step 4: Bring data, not opinions.

Annual Reset should be evidence-based:

- Customer feedback themes from the past year
- NPS/CSAT trends
- Support ticket analysis (what are customers expecting that we're not delivering?)
- Sales win/loss analysis (what promises closed deals vs. lost them?)
- Gate approval/denial log
- Drift Audit findings

Data makes the conversation concrete instead of abstract strategic planning.

Step 5: End with commitments, not ideas.

Annual Reset should produce decisions:

- "Our Core Promise remains [X]" or "Our Core Promise is changing to [Y] effective Q2"
- "We're moving these 4 promises from Supporting to Conditional"
- "We're killing these 6 Legacy promises by end of Q1"
- "We're adding this new Gate question based on last year's patterns"

Commitments > insights. If you leave without decisions, the Reset didn't work.

What success looks like: Annual Promise Reset happens every year, on schedule, with full leadership attendance. You leave with clear decisions about Core Promise, Stack changes, and Gate calibration. The Reset prevents annual drift accumulation.

***

Challenge #5: Distributed Teams Don't Participate in the Rhythm

What this looks like:

Your Austin headquarters team has solid Alignment Rhythm. Weekly Standups run smoothly. Monthly Stack Reviews happen. But your offshore team in Manila? They've never attended a Standup. They don't know when Stack Reviews happen. Quarterly Gate Calibration doesn't include them.

You have rhythm at HQ. You have chaos everywhere else.

Why this happens:

Time zones make synchronous participation hard. Or you never extended the invitation to distributed teams. Or they weren't trained on how to participate. Or they assume "Alignment Rhythm" is an HQ thing that doesn't apply to them.

The result: distributed teams operate on outdated Stacks, spot drift but don't report it, and make promises no one at HQ knows about.

How to resolve it:

Step 1: Make Weekly Standups asynchronous for distributed teams.

Don't force Manila team to join at 2am their time. Create an async alternative:

Async Standup format:

- Dedicated Slack channel: #promise-standup
- Every Monday, each person posts their three updates (drift spotted, decisions needed, Stack suggestions)
- HQ team reads and responds within 24 hours
- If something needs discussion, schedule a focused 15-minute call

Async isn't perfect, but it's better than exclusion.

Step 2: Rotate Monthly Stack Review timing.

One month, schedule it for Manila-friendly time (early morning Austin, end-of-day Manila). Next month, Austin-friendly time. Alternate.

This is inconvenient for everyone sometimes, which means it's fair. And it ensures distributed teams can attend at least half the Reviews.

Step 3: Record all Rhythm meetings and share within 24 hours.

Even if distributed teams can't attend live, they should see what happened:

- Record Monthly Stack Review
- Share recording + written summary within 24 hours
- Give distributed teams 48 hours to respond with input

Their input might be asynchronous, but it's still included.

Step 4: Assign distributed team representatives to Gate Committee.

Don't make the Gate an HQ-only decision. If Manila team is a major promise keeper, they need a voice in what promises get approved.

Rotate a Manila team member onto the Gate Committee for 6-month terms. They can participate via video for urgent decisions, async for routine ones.

Step 5: Hold Annual Promise Reset with distributed teams included.

If you can't get everyone in one location, do hybrid:

- HQ team in conference room
- Distributed teams join via video (high-quality setup, not just laptop cameras)
- Facilitator ensures remote participants get equal airtime

Or alternate years: this year in Austin, next year in Manila, etc.

Step 6: Create a shared Rhythm calendar visible to all teams.

Distributed teams shouldn't have to guess when Alignment Rhythm events happen. Create a shared calendar:

- Weekly Standups (with async option noted)
- Monthly Stack Review dates and times
- Quarterly Gate Calibration dates
- Annual Promise Reset

Make it visible in Slack, email signatures, and team dashboards.

What success looks like: Distributed teams participate in Alignment Rhythm (synchronously when possible, asynchronously when necessary).

They spot drift and report it. They attend Stack Reviews. They have representation in Gate decisions. Geographic distribution doesn't create alignment gaps.

162

Next: In Chapter 5, you'll activate your Alignment Network — every human, system, and AI that keeps your promises.

FIVE

THE ALIGNMENT NETWORK

"We've doubled our team size in six months," Maria told Marcus in Chapter 13. *"Not because business is growing. Because confusion is growing."*

That sentence stopped the room.

The offshore team in Manila wasn't failing. They were working harder than anyone at headquarters — covering extra shifts, fielding escalations at 2 AM, answering questions about features that didn't exist, trying to keep promises they'd never been told were the promises. They weren't a weak link. They were a strong link operating in the dark.

Your Alignment Network is every person, system, and AI that makes or keeps a promise on your company's behalf. When it's aligned, you have leverage. When it's not, you have Maria's situation: good people doing heroic work to compensate for a system that never gave them what they needed.

Here's how to change that.

What the Alignment Network Is

Your Alignment Network includes every person, system, and technology that touches customer expectations.

When aligned, it becomes your competitive advantage.

When misaligned, it becomes your source of chaos.

The Alignment Network includes:

Department Keepers:

- Sales, Marketing, Product, Engineering, Delivery, Support, Customer Success, Operations, Documentation teams, QA, Legal, Finance, Leadership, Field teams

System Keepers:

- Automations, workflows, templates, CRM sequences, subscription flows, pricing rules, QA rules, AI agent triggers

Offshore & Global Teams:

- Support teams, operational backbone, BPO partners

AI Keepers:

- Chatbots, AI assistants, training datasets, workflow triggers, autogenerated messaging

Documentation Keepers:

- Knowledge bases, internal wikis, SOPs, training docs, onboarding tools, third-party help centers

Silent Keepers (the ones companies forget):

- Cached old web pages, third-party listings, comparison sites, long-tail blog content, AI models trained on old truth, rogue PDFs, legacy sales decks, archived files

These Silent Keepers are some of the most dangerous sources of Promise Drift.

Why the Alignment Network Matters

Customers don't care who created the misalignment.

If Support says something different from Marketing...

If Offshore contradicts Onshore...

If AI explains things incorrectly...

If Delivery can't fulfill Sales' promises...

If documentation is outdated...

The customer sees only one company. To them, inconsistency = dishonesty. Even if it wasn't intentional.

The Alignment Network ensures every promise is clear, consistent, aligned, deliverable, reinforced, documented, governed, trained, and updated.

The 6 Keeper Categories

PAS organizes all Promise Keepers into six categories:

1. Organization Department Keepers

- **Sales** — Must stay within the Stack
- **Marketing** — Must use Gate-approved language
- **Product/Engineering** — Must define truth boundaries
- **Delivery/Onboarding** — Keeps the operational promises
- **Support** — Keeps the "reality experience" aligned with the promised experience
- **Customer Success** — Manages expectations over time
- **Field Teams/Retail Staff** — Keep the in-person experience consistent

Alignment Tools:

- Allowed Promises List
- Gate training
- Stack training
- Weekly Promise Standups

2. System Keepers

Systems keep promises automatically — or break them accidentally.

Examples: automated emails, onboarding workflows, CRM sequences, subscription flows, pricing rules, QA rules, AI agent triggers

The rule: Systems must be reviewed quarterly during Gate Calibration.

If your automation says, "Expect activation in 24 hours" and activation takes 72 hours... you just made a promise you cannot keep.

3. Offshore & Global Teams

Global teams are often:

- The main support force
- The main operational backbone
- Handling 60-90% of customer interactions
- Operating without full context

If they're not aligned, the company can't be aligned.

PAS Rules for Offshore Alignment:

- They must participate in the Alignment Network
- They must have access to Stack updates
- They must stop guessing
- They must flag drift when they detect it
- They must be included in Promise Standups
- They must receive the same training and truth as onshore teams

Your global teams are not "afterthoughts." They are Promise Keepers.

4. AI Keepers

AI — when aligned — becomes the most consistent Promise Keeper in your entire organization.

AI — when unaligned — becomes the fastest creator of drift.

AI must be:

- Trained exclusively on the Promise Stack

- Constrained with Gate-approved language
- Stripped of legacy data
- Corrected weekly
- Monitored for hallucinations
- Updated immediately when promises change
- Reviewed by a Gatekeeper before deployment

AI now generates customer answers, sales copy, onboarding instructions, support suggestions, marketing content, and product documentation.

This makes AI a core component of promise-keeping, not an accessory.

5. Documentation Keepers

Documentation is one of the biggest causes of Promise Drift.

Examples: old KB articles, outdated onboarding docs, internal wikis that employees still reference, third-party help centers, "tribal knowledge" documents, PDFs created years ago

In PAS, documentation has an owner.

Doc Owners must:

- Attend Alignment Rhythm meetings
- Update public and internal docs monthly
- Eliminate legacy content
- Ensure AI models only reference current truth
- Centralize documentation in one place

Documentation is not paperwork. Documentation is how promises get transmitted at scale.

6. Leadership Keepers

Leaders are the most powerful Promise Keepers — and promise breakers.

When leaders get excited, riff on ideas, speak aspirationally, present

visionary thinking, hint at future capabilities, or talk loosely about strategy...
employees treat these as promises, not concepts.

Leadership must:

- Route ideas through the Gate
- Label future thinking as "not a promise"
- Reinforce the Core Promise
- Model clarity
- Ask "Is that a promise?" in meetings
- Avoid improvisation in public
- Protect the Alignment Network

A leader who speaks loosely creates exponential drift.

A leader who speaks clearly creates exponential trust.

How to Align the Alignment Network

Step 1: Map Your Keepers

List every keeper category:

- Organization Department Leaders
- AI
- Offshore
- Systems
- Docs
- Partners

This reveals gaps.

Step 2: Train Every Keeper on the Stack

Every keeper must know:

- The Core Promise

- All Supporting Promises
- Which promises are Conditional
- Which are Experimental
- What has been retired

This turns knowledge into alignment.

Before Marcus included the offshore teams in Chapter 13, Maria's team in Manila and Paolo's team in Bogotá had been answering customer questions without ever seeing the Promise Stack. They were following documentation that hadn't been updated. They were fielding escalations at 1:47 AM, 2:13 AM, 3:06 AM — guessing at what was real. Stack training didn't just give them information. It gave them something to stand on.

Step 3: Assign Each Keeper a Promise Role

Examples:

- **Sales:** Only use Gate-approved language
- **Marketing:** Validate every claim through the Stack
- **Documentation:** Update truth monthly
- **AI:** Respond only with Stack-approved content
- **Offshore:** Flag drift immediately
- **Leadership:** Protect clarity at all costs

Step 4: Install Keeper Feedback Loops

Each Keeper must have a clear way to report:

- Drift sightings
- Broken promises
- Confusing language
- Outdated claims
- Customer misinterpretations

These feed the Gate and the Rhythm.

The feedback loop Marcus created with the offshore teams is what made Week 8 possible. When Maria pinged the leadership channel about "hyper-flex automation," she wasn't breaking protocol — she was using exactly the channel Marcus had promised her in Chapter 13: "You see it, you say it. No hierarchy. No permission needed." Without that channel, the LinkedIn ad would have kept running.

Step 5: Build the Keeper Scorecard

Track:

- Consistency
- Accuracy
- Alignment
- Customer impact
- Drift reduction
- Documentation hygiene
- AI stability

Scorecards make alignment measurable.

Common Challenges When
Aligning Your Alignment Network

Your Alignment Network—the people and systems that actually keep your promises—is often invisible until it breaks. Here's how to identify, train, and align the keepers who make or break customer experience.

Challenge #1: You Can't Identify
All Your Promise Keepers

What this looks like:

You start mapping your Alignment Network. The obvious ones are easy: support team, delivery team, sales. But then you realize:

     THE ALIGNMENT NETWORK

Your AI chatbot is making promises. Who owns that?

Your automated email sequences make commitments. Who's responsible?

Your knowledge base has outdated information. Who maintains it?

Your partner network represents you to customers. Are they keepers?

Your offshore contractors answer questions. Do they count?

You thought you had 20 promise keepers. You actually have 200+ touch-points where promises get made or kept, and you can't identify who's responsible for half of them.

Why this happens:

Promise-keeping has become distributed and automated. It's not just humans anymore. Systems, AI, third parties, and legacy automation all make commitments on your behalf—often without anyone explicitly owning them.

How to resolve it:

Step 1: Map every customer touchpoint, not just every team.

Don't start with "who are our people?" Start with "where do customers encounter promises?"

Trace the customer journey:

- **Awareness stage:** Website, ads, social media, content, review sites
- **Evaluation stage:** Sales calls, demos, proposals, pricing pages
- **Purchase stage:** Checkout flow, terms of service, order confirmations
- **Onboarding stage:** Welcome emails, setup guides, training materials
- **Usage stage:** Product interface, help docs, chatbots, in-app messaging
- **Support stage:** Tickets, chat, phone, email, community forums
- **Renewal stage:** Account reviews, upgrade offers, retention campaigns

Every touchpoint is a promise-making or promise-keeping moment. List them all.

Step 2: For each touchpoint, ask: "What system or person controls this?"

- Website content → Marketing team (human keeper)
- AI chatbot responses → Product team + AI system (hybrid keeper)
- Automated emails → Marketing ops + email platform (hybrid keeper)
- Support tickets → Support team + ticketing system (hybrid keeper)
- Knowledge base → Support + documentation team (human keeper)
- Partner communications → Partner team + partners themselves (third-party keeper)

Some touchpoints have clear owners. Some don't. The ones without owners are your biggest drift risk.

Step 3: Assign explicit ownership to orphaned touchpoints.

For every touchpoint without a clear keeper, assign one:

- "AI chatbot responses: Product team owns the training data, reviews responses quarterly, and maintains alignment with Stack."
- "Automated email sequences: Marketing ops owns the content, reviews against Stack monthly, updates broken promises within 48 hours."
- "Partner communications: Partner team owns training materials, reviews partner messaging quarterly, provides Stack updates whenever it changes."

Ownership means: someone is accountable for keeping this touchpoint aligned with your promises.

Step 4: Distinguish between Keeper types.

Not all keepers are equal. Categorize them:

- **Direct Keepers:** Your employees who make/keep promises (support, sales, delivery)
- **System Keepers:** Automated systems under your control (chatbot, emails, product interface)

- **Third-Party Keepers:** External people/systems representing you (partners, resellers, contractors, offshore teams)
- **Legacy Keepers:** Documentation, old content, archived materials that customers still find

Each type needs different alignment approaches.

Step 5: Don't try to train everyone at once.

Start with Direct Keepers (your employees). Get them aligned first.

Then tackle System Keepers (AI, automation).

Then Third-Party Keepers (partners, contractors).

Finally, audit and update Legacy Keepers (old content).

Trying to align 200 touchpoints simultaneously is overwhelming. Sequence it.

What success looks like: You have a complete map of every customer touchpoint. Each touchpoint has an assigned keeper. No orphaned systems making promises without accountability.

<hr>

Challenge #2: Offshore or Distributed Teams Aren't Aligned With HQ

What this looks like:

Your Austin team just updated the Stack. Your Manila offshore support team is still using promises from two quarters ago. When customers contact Manila support, they get different answers than when they contact Austin.

You discover this when a customer says: "Your Manila team told me I'd get X, but your Austin team says that's not available."

You don't have one Alignment Network. You have multiple networks operating independently.

Why this happens:

Time zones make training hard. Documentation gets updated at HQ but doesn't reach offshore teams. Language barriers create interpretation gaps. Or offshore teams were simply never included in the Alignment Network training.

How to resolve it:

Step 1: Include offshore teams in Stack creation from day one.

Don't build the Stack at HQ and "roll it out" to offshore. Bring offshore representatives into Stack-building sessions.

Why? They know what customers actually ask for. They know what's deliverable. They know where promises break. They're not just implementers—they're essential sources of truth.

Step 2: Create a single, live Stack document accessible to all teams.

No PDFs. No printed handouts. No emailed snapshots.

One Google Doc (or equivalent) that:

- HQ and offshore teams both access
- Updates in real-time when Stack changes
- Shows version history (what changed and when)
- Is the definitive source of truth

When the Stack changes, it changes for everyone simultaneously.

Step 3: Translate for language, not for interpretation.

If your offshore team operates in a different language, translate the Stack word-for-word. Don't let teams "adapt it to local market."

The Core Promise is the same in Manila as Austin. Supporting Promises don't change based on geography.

"Local adaptation" = local drift. Translate literally.

Step 4: Schedule dedicated offshore training sessions.

Don't just send them the updated Stack and hope they read it. Schedule training:

When Stack changes:

- 30-minute live session (or recorded if time zones impossible)
- Walk through what changed and why
- Answer questions in real-time
- Provide scenarios: "Customer asks for X, how do you respond?"

Quarterly refresher:

- Review entire Stack (not just changes)
- Test understanding with role-play scenarios
- Update any scripts or templates

Step 5: Create an offshore-to-HQ feedback channel.

Offshore teams spot drift first. They hear customer confusion. They get asked for promises not in the Stack. They see where documentation contradicts reality.

Make it easy to report:

- Dedicated Slack channel: #offshore-drift-reports
- Weekly Standup agenda item for offshore findings
- Monthly call specifically for offshore team to flag misalignments

When Manila says "customers keep asking for X but it's not in our Stack," that's gold. Act on it.

Step 6: Audit offshore-specific materials quarterly.

Your main website might be updated, but offshore teams often have:

- Regional knowledge base articles
- Translated documentation
- Chat scripts and canned responses
- Email templates
- Training materials

These lag behind HQ updates. Audit them specifically every quarter and align to current Stack.

What success looks like: Offshore team can recite the Core Promise. They operate from the same Stack as HQ. When Stack changes, they're trained within 48 hours. Customer experience is consistent regardless of which team they reach.

Challenge #3: Your AI Systems Keep Making Promises You Never Approved

What this looks like:

You discover your AI chatbot has been telling customers:

- "We offer 24/7 phone support" (you don't)
- "Setup takes 10 minutes" (it takes 2-3 hours)
- "All features available on all plans" (features are tiered)
- "Customization included at no cost" (customization requires professional services fee)

None of these promises are in your Stack. None were approved by the Gate. But the AI has been confidently making them for months.

Why this happens:

AI systems are trained on historical data—old websites, old documentation, old support conversations. They learn patterns from when promises were different.

Or the AI hallucinates based on what seems reasonable. Or it was trained on competitor content and adopted their promises.

Nobody is explicitly managing what the AI is allowed to promise.

How to resolve it:

Step 1: Audit your AI's actual outputs, not just its training.

Don't assume the AI is saying what you think it's saying. Review real conversations:

- Pull 100 recent chatbot conversations
- Read them specifically for promises made
- Flag any promise not in your Stack
- Categorize: accurate, outdated, hallucinated, or competitor-borrowed

You can't fix what you haven't seen.

Step 2: Explicitly train AI on your current Stack.

Don't rely on general training. Give your AI specific Stack training:

"Our Core Promise is: [exact text]"

"Our Supporting Promises are: [exact list]"

"Promises we do NOT make: [explicit exclusions]"

"If asked about [X], respond with: [approved language]"

The more explicit your training, the less the AI drifts.

Step 3: Build guardrails for common drift patterns.

If your AI keeps promising things you don't offer, add explicit constraints:

"Never promise 24/7 support. Our support hours are 9am-6pm ET Monday-Friday."

"Never promise custom development. Direct users to professional services for customization."

"Never promise pricing. Direct users to sales team or pricing page."

Explicit "never" rules prevent drift in high-risk areas.

Step 4: Review and update AI training quarterly.

AI doesn't stay aligned automatically. Every time your Stack changes, update AI training:

- New Supporting Promise added? Train AI to offer it.

- Legacy Promise killed? Train AI to stop mentioning it.
- Conditional Promise modified? Update AI's conditions.

Set a quarterly review: "Does our AI's training match our current Stack?"

Step 5: Monitor AI outputs continuously.

Don't audit AI quarterly and assume it stays aligned. Monitor ongoing:

- Flag conversations where AI makes promises
- Compare flagged promises against Stack
- When drift detected, retrain immediately

Some companies assign someone to spot-check 10 AI conversations daily. Five minutes of review catches drift before it compounds.

Step 6: Make AI limitations visible to customers.

If your AI can't reliably stay aligned (and many can't), make that clear:

"This is an AI assistant. For definitive answers about our services and commitments, please contact our support team."

Customers should know they're talking to AI, not a human keeper who's accountable for accuracy.

What success looks like: Your AI makes promises that align with your Stack. When Stack changes, AI training updates within one week. Drift gets caught and corrected within days, not months.

Challenge #4: Documentation Team Can't Keep Up With Stack Changes

What this looks like:

Marketing updates a promise. Sales adjusts terms. Product ships a feature. The Stack gets updated in real-time.

But your documentation team is 3 months behind. They're still writing help articles, updating knowledge base, revising training materials for promises that changed last quarter.

Customers read outdated docs. Support team follows outdated scripts. New employees get trained on outdated promises.

Why this happens:

Documentation is chronically under-resourced. One person (or small team) is trying to maintain hundreds of articles, guides, scripts, and training materials across multiple platforms.

When the Stack changes, documentation update is treated as "we'll get to it eventually." But eventually is too late—customers are reading the old promises right now.

How to resolve it:

Step 1: Triage documentation by customer visibility.

Not all documentation is equal. Prioritize by impact:

Tier 1 (Update within 48 hours):

- Customer-facing website pages
- Pricing page
- Terms of service
- Top 10 help articles (most-viewed)
- AI chatbot training data

Tier 2 (Update within 2 weeks):

- Full knowledge base
- Sales collateral
- Support scripts
- Onboarding materials

Tier 3 (Update within 30 days):

- Internal training materials
- Archived content
- Secondary support docs

When Stack changes, Tier 1 gets updated immediately. Tier 2 and 3 follow.

Step 2: Make documentation updates part of Stack change workflow.

Don't treat documentation as a separate step. Make it required:

"To add a new Supporting Promise to the Stack, you must:

1. Get Gate approval
2. Update the Stack document
3. **Update Tier 1 documentation within 48 hours**
4. Submit Tier 2/3 update requests to documentation team"

No Stack change is complete until customer-facing docs are updated.

Step 3: Give documentation team access to Stack change log.

Documentation team shouldn't have to hunt for changes. Create a Stack change log:

- What changed (promise added/modified/removed)
- Date changed
- Which documentation needs updating
- Priority tier

Documentation team reviews this log weekly and works through updates systematically.

Step 4: Empower non-documentation team to update Tier 1.

Don't bottleneck everything through one documentation team. Empower:

- Marketing to update marketing pages
- Sales to update sales collateral
- Product to update product docs
- Support to update top support articles

　　　　　　　　　THE ALIGNMENT NETWORK

Documentation team provides templates and review, but doesn't personally update everything.

Step 5: Audit for stale content quarterly.

Even with best efforts, some documentation will lag. Quarterly audit:

- Search your site for legacy promise language
- Review oldest knowledge base articles (haven't been updated in 6+ months)
- Check automated email sequences for outdated commitments
- Review partner-facing materials

Flag anything misaligned with current Stack and update or archive it.

Step 6: When in doubt, archive rather than leave outdated.

If documentation team can't update an old article quickly, archive it. Better to have no information than wrong information.

Outdated promises hurt more than missing documentation.

What success looks like: When Stack changes, Tier 1 documentation updates within 48 hours. Documentation team has a clear change log to work from. Customers rarely encounter outdated promises in help content.

Challenge #5: You Train Keepers Once, Then They Drift Back to Old Habits

What this looks like:

You do comprehensive Alignment Network training. Everyone learns the Stack. Support team understands Core Promise. Sales knows which promises need Gate approval.

For two weeks, it's perfect. Then:

Support starts making promises off-Stack again. "I know we're not supposed to promise same-day shipping, but the customer was upset, so I said we'd try."

Sales bypasses the Gate. "The deal was closing, I didn't have time to check. I figured it was fine."

Slowly, everyone reverts to pre-PAS habits.

Why this happens:

Training provides knowledge. But behavior change requires reinforcement. Without ongoing accountability and reinforcement, people default to what's familiar—even if it creates drift.

One-time training doesn't create lasting change.

How to resolve it:

Step 1: Make the Stack visible everywhere.

Don't make people remember training. Make the Stack impossible to ignore:

- Poster in support team area: "Our Core Promise: [text]"
- Sales CRM pop-up before closing deals: "Have you checked this against the Stack?"
- Support ticket system: Link to Stack at top of interface
- New hire onboarding: Stack is Day 1 content
- Email signatures: Link to Stack document

When the Stack is everywhere, people reference it instead of guessing.

Step 2: Catch drift in real-time, not in quarterly reviews.

Don't wait for monthly Stack Review to discover drift. Catch it daily:

- Manager spot-checks 3-5 support conversations daily for promise alignment
- Sales manager reviews proposals before they're sent
- Marketing manager reviews campaigns before launch

THE ALIGNMENT NETWORK

When someone drifts, correct it immediately: "I see you promised X. That's not in our Stack. Here's what we can promise instead."

Step 3: Celebrate alignment, not just correct drift.

Don't only give feedback when people drift. Recognize when they stay aligned:

"Great job checking the Stack before responding. You could have promised same-day delivery but correctly offered 2-day instead."

Positive reinforcement sustains behavior change better than only correcting mistakes.

Step 4: Make Stack refresher training quarterly.

Don't assume one training lasts forever. Schedule quarterly refreshers:

- 30-minute session reviewing Stack (especially any changes)
- Role-play scenarios: "Customer asks for X, what do you say?"
- Q&A: "What promises are you unsure about?"

Quarterly refreshers prevent drift creep.

Step 5: Include Stack alignment in performance reviews.

If staying aligned doesn't affect performance evaluation, people won't prioritize it.

Add to review criteria:

- "Consistently makes promises aligned with Stack"
- "Uses Gate process appropriately before committing to new promises"
- "Spots and reports drift when discovered"

What gets measured gets managed.

Step 6: Make Stack violations visible (not punitive, but visible).

Track drift instances:

- "This week: 3 instances of off-Stack promises (down from 7 last week)"

Make progress visible. Teams want to see the number go down.

Don't punish individual drift (that creates hiding). Measure team progress toward alignment.

What success looks like: Keepers reference the Stack routinely, not just during training. Drift gets caught and corrected in real-time. Alignment improves monthly. The Stack becomes "how we work," not "what we were trained on once."

Why the Alignment Network Works

Because it upgrades your entire company from:

- Opinion-driven → truth-driven
- Siloed → connected
- Improvisational → consistent
- Confusing → predictable
- Fragile → scalable

And it recognizes the new reality: In the modern world, promises are kept by systems, not just people.

When your Alignment Network is aligned, your company becomes unstoppable.

Next: In Chapter 6, you'll run the Drift Audit — finding and fixing misalignment before it harms the business.

Worksheet: Alignment Network Map

A. Organization Department Keepers (list roles and names):

B. System Keepers:

C. Offshore Keepers:

D. AI Keepers:

E. Documentation Keepers:

F. Leadership Keepers:

G. Gaps Identified:

H. Alignment Actions:

SIX

THE DRIFT AUDIT

Chapter 11 was AxisLine's reckoning. The Drift Audit revealed promises hiding everywhere:

Their AI chatbot was guaranteeing 'predictive scheduling' that the platform didn't offer. **Their legacy website** promised "24/7 phone support" they'd discontinued eight months earlier. **Their sales decks** included screenshots of features that had been sunset. **Their offshore knowledge base** contradicted current policy. **Their automated email sequences** referenced a pricing structure they no longer offered.

The team stood in front of hundreds of sticky notes—a mosaic of truth, a map of drift, a mirror no one had expected. Marcus's first reaction was panic. *How did we let this happen?* Victor's response was calm: "This happens to every company. You're not broken. You're just growing without a system."

The Drift Audit isn't about shame—it's about awareness. You can't fix what you can't see. And most companies are making hundreds of promises they don't even know about.

Before AxisLine could fix anything, they had to see everything. That's what the Drift Audit does. Not to indict your company — but to illuminate it.

What Is Drift?

Drift = The gap between what your company says and what your company does.

It forms in four ways:

1. **Upward Drift** — Teams promise more than operations can deliver
2. **Downward Drift** — Teams promise less than the company is capable of
3. **Side Drift** — Different teams communicate different expectations

4. **Legacy Drift** — Outdated information continues influencing perceptions

All four hurt trust.

What the Drift Audit Does

The Drift Audit is a structured assessment that reviews:

- Written promises
- Spoken promises
- Implied promises
- Automated promises
- AI-generated promises
- Operational realities

It gives you a clear map of what's aligned, what's misaligned, why the drift occurred, how severe it is, who is affected, and what needs to be updated, retired, or recalibrated.

You cannot run the Promise Alignment System without auditing drift.

The 5 Audit Zones

Drift appears in five predictable places:

1. Sales & Marketing Drift (Expectation Drift)

This is where most drift originates.

Causes:

- Optimistic claims
- Outdated messaging
- Stretch promises
- Inconsistent demos
- "We can probably do this" statements

- Legacy landing pages still indexed
- Freelancers or agencies reusing old copy

Audit Steps:

- Review all sales scripts
- Review proposal templates
- Review outbound sequences
- Review landing pages & paid ads
- Review demo narration
- Review webinar claims
- Review customer-facing decks

Key question: "Do our words match our reality?"

2. Product & Capability Drift (Feasibility Drift)

Causes:

- Features are unclear
- Capabilities are over-interpreted
- Roadmap items are mistaken for commitments
- Beta features seep beyond intended audiences
- Product teams assume "future state" as "current state"

Audit Steps:

- Review feature list
- Review roadmap communication
- Review product marketing
- Review onboarding expectations
- Review integration capabilities
- Review limitations not clearly expressed

Key question: "Are customers expecting capabilities we don't support?"

3. Delivery & Support Drift (Experience Drift)

Causes:

- Onboarding timelines vary
- Outcomes differ by customer
- Support answers are inconsistent
- Offshore teams interpret instructions differently
- Undocumented edge cases appear
- Service levels are not standardized

Audit Steps:

- Review support transcripts
- Review onboarding calls
- Review escalation data
- Shadow customer success calls
- Interview delivery teams
- Ask offshore teams what confuses them

Key question: "Does the experience match the promise?"

4. Documentation (Knowledge Drift)

This is the silent killer.

Causes:

- Old knowledge base articles
- Outdated standard operating procedures (SOPs)
- Internal wikis storing legacy truths
- PDFs from previous leaders circulating
- Slack threads that become "informal instructions"
- Outdated onboarding materials
- Playbooks referencing old workflows

Audit Steps:

- Evaluate internal and external documentation
- Look for dates hidden on page bottoms
- Review "shadow documentation" (Google Drive, Notion, old HR systems)
- Check partner documents
- Check old blog posts
- Purge outdated materials

Key question: "Are there "old truths" still alive anywhere?"

5. AI & Automation Drift
(Generative & System Drift)

AI creates drift when:

- Trained on outdated content
- Using fuzzy language
- Generalizing future promises
- Offering workarounds that don't exist
- Hallucinating capabilities that don't exist

Automation creates drift when:

- Triggers use legacy timelines
- Emails promise incorrect delivery dates
- Sequences reference previous features
- Workflows assume outdated behavior and processes

Audit Steps:

- Review chatbot transcripts
- Define guardrails and develop "golden test set"
- Review AI outputs regularly and test updated models internally before launching
- Audit email flows
- Audit CRM sequences

- Audit notifications and automated instructions
- Review content AI uses for training

Key question: "Do our systems say things our team members no longer say?"

The Drift Audit Process

Step 1: Collect Everything

Gather every source of truth:

- Copy, scripts, docs, emails, templates
- Onboarding flows, support transcripts
- AI responses, offshore materials
- Older versions of pages
- Internal shared files
- Social media messaging

This is the "truth dump."

Step 2: Compare Against the Promise Stack

Check each item:

- Is this a Core Promise?
- Is it a Supporting Promise?
- Is it Conditional?
- Is it Experimental?
- Is it Legacy?

Anything outside the Stack is drift.

Step 3: Classify the Drift by Type

Mark each issue as:

- Upward
- Downward
- Side
- Legacy

Step 4: Assign Severity

- **S1 — Critical Drift:** Breaks the Core Promise and creates customer harm.
- **S2 — Serious Drift:** Breaks Supporting Promises and creates misalignment.
- **S3 — Moderate Drift:** Barely misaligned but recurring.
- **S4 — Minor Drift:** Small miscommunication.
- **S5 — Cosmetic Drift:** Won't affect customers but should be corrected.

At AxisLine, the AI chatbot promising "predictive scheduling" was the clearest S1 — it directly contradicted their Core Promise and was reaching customers daily. The legacy claim that "support is 24/7" — which had never been true — was S2: a Supporting Promise that set false expectations for every new customer who read it. The severity scale determines what you fix first. AxisLine fixed the AI first. That took four months and eleven iterations.

Step 5: Assign Ownership

Every drift item must have an owner from one of the Keeper categories.

When AxisLine ran their Drift Audit in Chapter 11, the most dangerous promises on the wall weren't the ones anyone had made deliberately — they were the ones no one had made deliberately. The AI chatbot promises. The legacy campaign claims. The features that had been sun-set but were still indexed. Those items had no owner. Victor's framework was simple: if it doesn't have a name next to it, it won't get fixed.

Step 6: Correct the Drift

Corrections can include:

- Update documentation
- Retrain AI models
- Revise scripts
- Retire legacy pages
- Replace outdated messaging
- Correct Sales language
- Clarify Conditional Promises
- Update product copy
- Adjust onboarding workflows

Step 7: Publish the Alignment Update

Three things must get updated:

- Humans
- Systems
- AI

This ensures that your "new truths" are articulated.

Common Challenges
When Running Drift Audits

The Drift Audit surfaces the gap between what you think you promise and what you actually promise. It's revealing, uncomfortable, and often overwhelming. Here's how to navigate the challenges that emerge.

Challenge #1: The Audit Reveals Hundreds
of Promises (Overwhelming Results)

What this looks like:

You run your first Drift Audit. You expected to find 30-40 promises to organize. Instead, you find:

- 80+ promises on your website alone
- 30+ promises in marketing emails from the last quarter
- 25+ promises in sales proposals
- 40+ promises in your help center documentation
- 15+ promises your AI chatbot is making
- 20+ promises in offshore team scripts
- Dozens more in automated emails, onboarding flows, and legacy materials

You're staring at 250+ promises. Your team is paralyzed. Someone says: "This is impossible. We can't fix all of this."

Why this happens:

Companies accumulate promises over years without pruning. Every campaign adds promises. Every sales conversation adjusts them. Every new feature creates promises. Nothing ever gets removed.

The Drift Audit doesn't create the problem—it reveals what was always there, invisible and unmanaged.

How to resolve it:

Step 1: Remember that awareness is progress.

Before the audit, you had 250 unmanaged promises operating in the dark. Now you have 250 visible promises you can organize.

You're not worse off. You're better informed.

Don't let the scale paralyze you. The number isn't the problem—the invisibility was.

Step 2: Triage into three buckets immediately.

Don't try to perfect-sort all 250 promises into Stack layers. First, do a rough triage:

Bucket A: Obviously aligned with Core Promise (keep these)

Bucket B: Obviously contradicts Core Promise or is deprecated (kill these)

Bucket C: Unclear—needs discussion (defer these)

You can triage 250 promises into these three buckets in 2-3 hours. Most will be obviously A or B. Only 20-30% will be genuinely unclear (Bucket C).

Step 3: Kill Bucket B immediately (within one week).

Don't debate. Don't analyze. Don't delay.

If a promise is deprecated, contradicts your Core Promise, or references features you don't offer—kill it. Remove it from the website. Delete it from docs. Update the chatbot. Purge it from sales decks.

Bucket B might be 60-80 promises. Eliminating them quickly reduces your workload by 30%.

Step 4: Organize Bucket A into Stack layers over 2-4 weeks.

Now you're down to maybe 120 aligned promises that need Stack placement. This is manageable.

Don't do it all in one marathon session. Organize 20-30 promises per week over a month:

- Week 1: Core + Supporting Promises
- Week 2: Conditional Promises
- Week 3: Experimental Promises
- Week 4: Review and finalize

Step 5: Get help with Bucket C.

The 30-50 unclear promises are where you need cross-functional input. These are the judgment calls:

- "Is this promise still relevant?"
- "Should this be Supporting or Conditional?"
- "Can we actually deliver this?"

Schedule focused working sessions with stakeholders. One hour per session, tackle 10 promises. You'll resolve Bucket C in 3-5 meetings.

What success looks like: You move from 250 overwhelming promises to a managed Stack in 4-6 weeks. You didn't fix everything instantly, but you created order from chaos. The promises are visible, categorized, and under control.

Challenge #2: Team Wants to Quit After Seeing Audit Results

What this looks like:

You present the Drift Audit findings to your leadership team. The reaction isn't "let's fix this." It's:

"This is a disaster. How did we let it get this bad?"

"We're fundamentally broken as a company."

"This proves we don't know what we're doing."

"Maybe we should just start over."

Instead of energizing the team to fix drift, the audit demoralizes them. Some people want to quit the process entirely.

Why this happens:

The audit reveals years of accumulated misalignment in one overwhelming presentation. People see the gap between intention and reality and feel shame.

They thought they were running a tight operation. The audit proves otherwise. That's hard to accept.

How to resolve it:

Step 1: Normalize drift as universal, not personal failure.

Before presenting audit findings, frame them:

"Every company has drift. This isn't evidence that we're broken—it's evidence that we're growing without a system. Today, we're doing what most companies never do: making the invisible visible so we can fix it."

Drift isn't a character flaw. It's gravity. All companies drift without deliberate management.

Step 2: Show that finding drift is success, not failure.

Reframe the narrative:

"Six months ago, we had 200+ promises we didn't even know about. Customers were confused. Teams were apologizing. Today, we can see every promise we make. We know what to fix. That's not failure—that's progress."

The audit didn't create problems. It surfaced problems that were always there.

Step 3: Celebrate early wins from the audit.

Don't wait until everything is fixed. Celebrate quick wins:

"This week, we killed 15 Legacy promises from our website. Customers now see consistent information."

"We found our chatbot was promising features we don't have. We fixed it today. No more false expectations."

Small corrections compound. Show the team that progress is happening.

Step 4: Break the fix into phases so it feels achievable.

Don't present the audit as "here's 200 problems to solve." Present it as:

"Phase 1 (this month): Kill obviously deprecated promises - 60 promises

Phase 2 (next month): Organize aligned promises into Stack - 100 promises

Phase 3 (month 3): Resolve unclear promises - 40 promises"

Phases make the work feel manageable instead of infinite.

Step 5: Acknowledge that some drift will always exist.

Perfection isn't the goal. Management is.

"We'll never eliminate 100% of drift. New promises will emerge. The difference is: now we have a system to catch and correct it before it compounds."

This prevents the team from aiming for impossible perfection and burning out.

What success looks like: The team sees the audit as a clarifying moment, not a condemnation. They feel energized to fix problems, not demoralized by them. They understand drift is normal and fixable.

———

Challenge #3: You Can't Get Budget to Fix Everything the Audit Revealed

What this looks like:

The Drift Audit revealed that:

- Your website needs a complete content rewrite (estimated: $15,000)
- Your documentation is 18 months outdated (estimated: 40 hours of writing)
- Your chatbot needs retraining (estimated: $8,000)
- Your offshore team needs new scripts and training (estimated: 60 hours)
- Your video tutorials are obsolete and need to be reshot (estimated: $12,000)

Total estimated cost to fix all drift: $50,000+ and 200+ hours.

You don't have the budget. Leadership says: "We can't afford to fix everything. What do we do?"

Why this happens:

The audit revealed years of accumulated technical debt in promise-making. You can't fix years of neglect instantly—especially without dedicated budget.

But you can't do nothing, either. Drift compounds daily.

How to resolve it:

Step 1: Separate "must fix now" from "fix over time."

Not all drift is equally urgent. Triage by customer impact:

Tier 1: High-impact drift (fix within 30 days)

- Promises that are completely false (features you don't offer)
- Promises that create legal/compliance risk
- Promises on high-traffic pages (homepage, pricing, product pages)

These might be 20-30% of total drift but cause 80% of customer confusion.

Tier 2: Medium-impact drift (fix within 90 days)

- Promises that are outdated but not completely wrong
- Promises in documentation customers access occasionally
- Promises in low-traffic legacy content

Tier 3: Low-impact drift (fix within 6-12 months)

- Promises in archived content
- Promises in materials you're sunsetting anyway
- Promises that rarely surface

Fix Tier 1 immediately. Schedule Tier 2. Defer Tier 3.

Step 2: Focus on high-leverage fixes first.

Some fixes eliminate drift across multiple channels:

Example: Retraining your chatbot might cost $8,000, but it fixes drift in thousands of customer conversations. That's higher leverage than rewriting one blog post.

Prioritize fixes that:

- Touch the most customers
- Affect the most promise keepers
- Prevent the most confusion

Step 3: Fix what you can with internal resources.

Not everything requires external budget:

Internal fixes (zero budget):

- Delete deprecated promises from website (1-2 hours)
- Update FAQ answers (4-6 hours)
- Revise sales deck templates (2-3 hours)
- Update chatbot scripts yourself (if you have access)

You might eliminate 40% of drift with internal effort alone.

Step 4: Justify budget with customer impact data.

When you need budget, don't present it as "we need to fix our mistakes." Present it as "here's the cost of drift vs. the ROI of fixing it."

Example: "Our chatbot is promising features we don't have. This creates 15-20 confused customer conversations per week. Support spends 30 minutes each resolving the confusion. Cost: 10 hours/week = $20,000/year in wasted support time. Fixing the chatbot costs $8,000 one-time. ROI: 5 months."

Make the business case: drift has a measurable cost. Fixing it has measurable ROI.

Step 5: Accept that some drift will persist—and manage it.

You might not fix 100% of drift in year one. That's okay.

Flag what you can't fix yet:

- Add notes to outdated docs: "This article was written for Version 2.0 and will be updated in Q3."

- Train support on common drift points: "If customers ask about X, here's the reality..."

Acknowledged drift is better than invisible drift.

What success looks like: You fix Tier 1 drift immediately (high impact, low cost). You build a roadmap to fix Tier 2 over quarters. You acknowledge Tier 3 exists but defer it. Drift gets managed within budget constraints, not ignored.

<hr>

Challenge #4: Different Departments Disagree on What Counts as "Drift"

What this looks like:

You're reviewing the Drift Audit with cross-functional stakeholders. Marketing points to a promise on the sales deck: "This is drift—we don't offer same-day onboarding anymore."

Sales pushes back: "That's not drift. We still offer it—just for Enterprise tier."

Marketing: "But the deck doesn't say 'Enterprise only.'"

Sales: "Everyone knows Enterprise means premium service."

Product chimes in: "Actually, we deprecated same-day onboarding last quarter. Even Enterprise gets 3-day onboarding now."

Sales: "Since when?"

Three departments, three different understandings of the same promise. You can't even agree on what drift IS.

Why this happens:

Different departments have different information. Changes happen but don't propagate. Marketing sees the public-facing promise. Sales sees what they're selling. Product sees what they built. Nobody's information is complete.

How to resolve it:

Step 1: Use the Stack as the single source of truth.

Don't debate what's "true" based on memory or departmental perspective. Ask one question:

"Is this promise in our Stack?"

If yes → Not drift (assuming it's accurate)

If no → Drift (whether intentional or not)

If unclear → Stack needs updating to clarify

The Stack decides. Not opinions.

Step 2: Document "what we thought was true" vs. "what is actually true."

When departments disagree, create a simple comparison:

Promise in question: "Same-day onboarding available"

List out each department, what they think is true and the evidence they are referring to. For example:

Marketing believes it was deprecated last quarter based on product release notes.

Sales believes it is still available for Enterprise clients based on a sales deck from Q2.

Product says it never existed for any client tier based on system capabilities.

This surfaces the actual source of disagreement. Often, it's not opinion—it's outdated information.

Step 3: Verify with operational reality, not marketing claims.

When in doubt, test:

- Can delivery actually provide same-day onboarding?
- What's the average onboarding time for the last 20 Enterprise customers?
- What do support tickets reveal about actual experience?

Operational reality trumps what anyone "thinks" is true.

Step 4: Update the Stack based on findings.

When you resolve a disagreement, update the Stack immediately:

"Same-day onboarding: Removed from all tiers as of Q2 2025. Current promise: 3-business-day onboarding for all customers, including Enterprise."

Document it. Publish it. Make it official.

Step 5: Use disagreements to find systemic communication gaps.

If three departments have three different understandings of one promise, you have a communication problem beyond this specific promise.

Ask: "How do we ensure everyone knows when promises change?"

This might reveal:

- Product ships changes without notifying marketing
- Marketing updates website without telling sales
- Sales adjusts pitches without documenting them

Fix the communication flow, not just the individual promise.

What success looks like: When departments disagree about drift, you have a clear process to resolve it. The Stack is the referee. Operational reality is the evidence. Disagreements get documented, resolved, and used to improve communication flows.

Challenge #5: The Audit Becomes a Blame Game

What this looks like:

You present the Drift Audit findings. Instead of focusing on fixes, the meeting devolves into finger-pointing:

"Marketing promised features we can't deliver."

"That's because Product never told us what got deprecated."

"We sent release notes. Sales just ignored them."

"Support is the one telling customers we offer 24/7 service."

"Because that's what your chatbot promised them first."

Everyone's defending their department and blaming others. No one's taking responsibility. The audit becomes about who caused drift, not how to fix it.

Why this happens:

Drift feels like failure. When the audit exposes misalignment, people's first instinct is self-protection: "This wasn't my fault."

Departments have been operating in silos. Each sees their piece as correct and everyone else as wrong.

How to resolve it:

Step 1: Set ground rules before presenting audit findings.

Before sharing results, establish the frame:

"This audit will reveal drift. Some of it will be surprising. Some will be uncomfortable. Our job today isn't to assign blame—it's to understand what happened and fix it. Drift is a system problem, not a people problem."

Set the expectation: we're here to solve, not punish.

Step 2: Present drift as patterns, not individual failures.

Don't say: "Marketing promised same-day delivery on this campaign, which we can't deliver."

Say: "We found a pattern: promises change in Product but don't propagate to customer-facing channels. Example: same-day delivery."

Frame drift as a communication gap in the system, not a mistake by a person.

Step 3: Use "we" language, not "you" language.

Don't say: "You (Marketing) promised features we don't have."

Say: "We found promises on our website that don't match our current capabilities."

"We" creates collective ownership. "You" creates defensiveness.

Step 4: Focus on forward-looking fixes, not backward-looking fault.

When drift is identified, immediately pivot to: "How do we prevent this in the future?"

Not: "Why did this happen?" (backward, blame-focused)

But: "What system do we need so this doesn't happen again?" (forward, solution-focused)

Step 5: Acknowledge that everyone contributed to drift (including leadership).

If the CEO or leadership is present, they should model accountability:

"We've all contributed to this drift. I approved campaigns without ensuring delivery could support them. I let promises proliferate without a management system. This isn't about one department failing—it's about all of us operating without alignment. Now we're fixing it together."

When leadership takes responsibility, defensiveness decreases.

Step 6: Celebrate departments that found their own drift.

If marketing proactively flagged drift in their materials, celebrate it:

"Marketing audited their own campaigns and found 12 promises that needed updating. They're fixing them this week. This is exactly the ownership we need."

Reward transparency and self-correction. Punish hiding drift.

What success looks like: The audit conversation stays solution-focused. Departments collaborate to fix drift instead of defending positions. The team understands drift as a system failure that requires system solutions, not individual blame.

Worksheet: Drift Audit Template

A. Drift Items Found:

B. Type: (circle) Upward / Downward / Side / Legacy

C. Severity:

S1 / S2 / S3 / S4 / S5

D. Related Promise Layer:

Core / Supporting / Conditional / Experimental / Legacy

E. Owner:

F. Fix Required:

G. Customer Impact:

Why the Drift Audit Works

Because it exposes invisible misalignment.

It gives leaders clarity, confidence, control, insight, stability, and predictability.

It reduces confusion, customer frustration, rework, inconsistency, blame, improvisation, AI hallucinations, and employee burnout.

Drift will always exist — but with the Drift Audit, you finally see it. And once you see it, you can correct it.

Next: In Chapter 7, you'll discover what it means to become a Promise Company — where alignment becomes identity.

SEVEN
BECOMING A
PROMISE COMPANY

Six months after Victor first walked through AxisLine's door, Marcus did something he hadn't done in over a year: he walked through the office slowly.

Not because he was lost. Because he wanted to see it.

Jasmine, the onboarding specialist who'd been drowning in mismatched expectations, was laughing on a customer call. The support dashboard was green. The offshore team's Slack channel had helpful updates instead of 3 AM panic messages. A sales rep was checking the Gate checklist before sending a proposal — not because she was required to, but because she'd learned it protected her.

And on the wall, someone had put a sticky note over the old mission statement: *The company that keeps its word.*

Marcus didn't say anything. He just headed to the conference room for the Weekly Standup. Tessa was already there.

"Ready?" she asked.

"Ready," he said.

That's what a Promise Company looks like. Not a rebrand. Not a restructure. Not a new strategy deck. A team that knows what it stands for, delivers on it consistently, and builds a culture where keeping your word is simply how you operate.

This chapter is about how to become that company — and what changes when you do.

What a Promise Company Is

A Promise Company is an organization that:

- Says only what it can deliver
- Delivers exactly what it says
- Keeps promises across humans, teams, and AI
- Aligns its entire ecosystem to one truth
- Eliminates drift quickly
- Trains for clarity
- Builds trust deliberately
- Scales predictably

It's rare. It's valuable. And in a noisy world full of hype and exaggeration, it's magnetic.

The 7 Traits of a Promise Company

1. They Operate With One Truth

Most companies operate with dozens of "truths":

- Sales has one truth
- Marketing has another
- Support has another
- AI has its own truth
- Offshore teams inherit old truth
- Documentation reflects last year's truth
- Leadership speaks future truth

Promise Companies operate with one truth.

The Promise Stack is the source. Everything else downstream reflects it.

This creates consistency, predictability, customer confidence, easier decision-making, simpler scaling, and stronger culture.

    BECOMING A PROMISE COMPANY

2. They Correct Drift Quickly

Drift is not seen as failure — it's seen as a signal.

Promise Companies:

- Identify drift early
- Celebrate drift sightings
- Correct drift calmly
- Fix the root cause
- Update humans, systems, and AI
- Close internal knowledge gaps
- Reinforce the Gate

Drift doesn't linger. It doesn't compound. It doesn't surprise them.

They see it. They fix it. They move forward.

3. They Train Everyone — Not Just the Frontline

Most companies train Sales on pitches, Support on handling tickets, Marketing on brand, Product on features.

Promise Companies train everyone on:

- The Core Promise
- Supporting Promises
- Conditional Promises
- The Promise Gate
- The Alignment Rhythm
- The Alignment Network
- How to identify drift
- How to request clarity
- How to correct misalignment

Everyone speaks the same language.

Internally → alignment.

Externally → consistency.

4. They Treat AI as a Promise Keeper, Not a Tool

Most companies use AI reactively.

Promise Companies use AI intentionally:

- AI is trained only on the Promise Stack
- AI avoids legacy data
- AI is constrained to truth
- AI is monitored weekly
- AI gets updated with Stack changes
- AI is treated as a real Keeper, not a helper

AI becomes a force multiplier for alignment. It keeps promises faster, more consistently, with less fatigue, and at larger scale.

AI becomes, quite literally, a guardian of truth.

AxisLine's chatbot took eleven iterations to align. Each pass removed legacy training data, tightened guardrails, and closed another hallucination. By Chapter 17, the same system that had been confidently promising "predictive scheduling" and "hyper-flex automations" was giving answers Devon could demonstrate in a leadership meeting without flinching. Four months. Eleven iterations. It was worth every one.

5. They Favor Clarity Over Creativity

They believe:

Clear is kind.

Clear is scalable.

Clear is profitable.

Clear is powerful.

Clear wins.

Creativity has a place — but not at the expense of truth.

Promise Companies eliminate vague language, inflated claims, buzzwords, aspirational language used as fact, and "storytelling" that implies false capability.

Clarity becomes a competitive advantage. And customers feel it instantly.

6. They Commit to Sustainable Growth

Growth is not a scramble.

Growth is not a gamble.

Growth is not a "hero effort."

Promise Companies scale by:

- Keeping their promises
- Protecting the Gate
- Designing predictable delivery
- Ensuring global teams stay aligned
- Automating with accurate information
- Eliminating legacy promises
- Standardizing consistent outcomes

They don't grow by chasing opportunity. They grow by reinforcing their identity.

The numbers AxisLine presented to their board in Chapter 19 didn't come from a new product or a new hire: NPS up from 27 to 48. Customer retention up 18%. Support tickets down 31%. Sales cycle shorter by two weeks. And the offshore team — which had added two extra shifts just to handle the confusion created by drift — reduced back to their core team. Every one of those results came from keeping the promises they'd already made.

7. They Protect Their Culture With Discipline

A culture of promise-keeping doesn't happen because leaders say, "We care about customers" or "We value integrity."

It happens because leaders:

- Model clarity
- Avoid improvisation
- Route promises through the Gate
- Speak in precise language
- Maintain the Alignment Rhythm
- Eliminate emotional guesswork
- Reinforce the Stack
- Correct drift respectfully
- Elevate Keepers across the organization

Promise-keeping becomes a norm. A habit. A muscle. A way of operating.

What Changes When You Become a Promise Company

Transformation 1: Employees Relax

They know what's true. They know what's expected. They know they won't be blamed for promises they didn't make.

Teams become calmer and more confident.

Transformation 2: Customers Trust Faster

When customers hear the same aligned message from Sales, Support, AI, Documentation, Website, Offshore teams, and Delivery... they start trusting earlier. And deeper.

Transformation 3: Leaders
Make Decisions Faster

Because everything goes through one lens: "Does this protect or dilute our Core Promise?"

This creates ruthless focus.

Transformation 4: AI Becomes a Strategic Asset

Instead of hallucinating, interpreting, exaggerating, and guessing...

AI becomes consistent, reliable, stable, aligned, and deeply helpful.

This is a huge competitive edge.

Transformation 5: Performance
Becomes Predictable

No more heroics. No more chaos. No more stress from broken expectations. No more surprises.

Predictability becomes the default. And predictability is the foundation of scale.

The Promise Company Maturity Model

Your organization is most likely between Levels 1-3 today. With dedication and intention, you can achieve Levels 4 and 5.

Level 1 — Promise Chaos

No Stack, no Gate, no Rhythm.

Level 2 — Promise Awareness

Teams recognize drift but don't know how to fix it.

Level 3 — Promise Hygiene

Some structure exists, but inconsistencies persist.

Level 4 — Promise System

Gate, Stack, Rhythm in place. Drift decreasing.

Level 5 — Promise Company

Alignment becomes identity. This is the ultimate goal of PAS.

The Promise Company Scorecard

Rate your company 1-5 on each dimension:

1. **One-Truth Alignment** — Do all teams share the same source of truth?
2. **Drift Detection Speed** — How quickly do you spot and correct misalignment?
3. **Alignment Network Clarity** — Are all Keepers clear on their roles?
4. **AI Alignment Strength** — Is AI trained and governed by the Promise Stack?
5. **Documentation Accuracy** — Are docs up-to-date and aligned?
6. **Sales & Marketing Consistency** — Do customer messages stay within the Gate?
7. **Global Team Alignment** — Are offshore teams delivering consistent expectations?
8. **Leadership Modeling** — Do leaders protect clarity and follow the Gate?
9. **Operational Predictability** — Does delivery reliably fulfill promises?
10. **Customer Trust** — Do customers feel you keep your word consistently?

Total Score:

- **10-19:** Promise Chaos
- **20-29:** Promise Awareness
- **30-36:** Promise Hygiene

- **37-43:** Promise System
- **44-50:** Promise Company

Next: In Chapter 8, you'll get the 90-Day Implementation Roadmap — the step-by-step plan to install PAS in your organization.

EIGHT

THE 90-DAY IMPLEMENTATION ROADMAP

AxisLine's transformation didn't happen in 90 days. In Chapter 15, Victor told them the truth: "Change is supposed to be messy. You've been drifting for years. Did you think you'd fix it in two weeks? This will take three months minimum."

He was being optimistic. **The real transformation took six months.**

Weeks 1-2: The team struggled to define their Core Promise and ran their first messy Drift Audit.

Weeks 3-6: Sales rebelled against the Gate. The AI kept hallucinating. The first Stack Review took 90 minutes instead of 15.

Week 6: Victor transitioned out, forcing the team to own the system themselves.

Weeks 7-12: The team wobbled but kept going. Small wins started appearing.

Months 4-6: The system clicked. NPS climbed. Teams relaxed. The culture shifted.

Your timeline will be similar. Not because you're slow—because real organizational change takes time. Habits need to form. Resistance needs to fade. New behaviors need to become automatic.

This roadmap gives you a realistic 90-day implementation plan—but understand that's just the foundation. Full transformation happens in months 4-6, when the system becomes part of how you operate, not something extra you do.

Here's how to start.

The PAS Installation Principles

Before we begin, four rules define successful execution:

1. **Start with truth, not aspiration.**
2. **Move fast — perfection slows alignment.**
3. **Train every Keeper — not just the front line.**
4. **Update humans, systems, and AI together.**

If you follow these four rules, PAS takes root quickly and permanently.

The 90-Day Roadmap (Overview)

Days 1-30 → Define and stabilize promise foundations

Days 31-60 → Install the systems that protect promises

Days 61-90 → Operationalize alignment across the Alignment Network

Let's walk through the plan step-by-step.

Days 1-30: Clarify Your Promises

This phase installs the foundation.

Step 1: Define the Core Promise

- Identify consistent outcomes
- Remove heroics
- Eliminate vague language
- Test feasibility with delivery & support
- Confirm with global teams & AI owners

Outcome: Your Core Promise is simple, real, and deliverable.

Step 2: Build the Promise Stack

Classify every promise into the five layers:

- Core
- Supporting
- Conditional
- Experimental
- Legacy

Outcome: You have a complete, accurate promise map.

Step 3: Run a Drift Audit

Audit the five Drift Zones:

1. Sales & Marketing
2. Product & Capability
3. Delivery & Support
4. Documentation & Knowledge
5. AI & Automation

Outcome: A list of alignment gaps and necessary corrections.

Step 4: Clean Legacy Drift

- Remove old PDFs
- Update website copy
- Purge outdated AI training content
- Correct documentation
- Retire old scripts

Outcome: You stop the old version of your company from speaking.

AxisLine retired 42 Legacy Promises in their first sorting session in Chapter 12. Some were retired quietly — deleted from documentation, removed from scripts. Others, like "unlimited automations" and "we integrate with anything," required public correction: updated FAQs, Support trained to handle the questions, the record set straight. Victor's instruction was specific: kill legacy promises clearly and publicly, or they keep haunting you.

Days 31-60: Protect Your Promises

This phase installs the governance layer.

Step 5: Install the Promise Gate

- Create the Drift Intake Form
- Form the Gate Committee
- Train all teams on Gate criteria
- Require Gate approval for new claims

Outcome: No new promises slip through.

Step 6: Publish the Allowed Promises List

This becomes the canonical truth for:

- Sales
- Marketing
- Product
- Support
- Offshore teams
- AI / automations
- Documentation
- Training

Outcome: All teams speak from the same truth.

Step 7: Activate the Alignment Rhythm

Install:

- Weekly Promise Standups
- Monthly Stack Reviews
- Quarterly Gate Calibration

Outcome: Drift is detected early and corrected quickly.

Days 61-90: Operationalize the Alignment Network

This phase makes alignment scalable across humans, systems, and AI.

Step 8: Train Every Keeper

Train:

- Sales, Marketing, Product, Engineering
- Support, Delivery, CS
- Offshore teams
- Documentation teams
- AI governance
- Leadership

Outcome: Everyone understands the Promise Stack, Gate, and Rhythm.

Step 9: Align Systems & AI

- Retrain AI on the Promise Stack
- Constrain chatbots
- Update automations
- Review CRM sequences
- Correct onboarding flows
- Align templates, emails, macros, and SOPs

Outcome: Systems stop making promises you can't keep.

This was AxisLine's longest step. Devon's team spent three days on the first retraining pass and the bot was still hallucinating — just more politely. The second attempt produced vague implications instead of direct hallucinations. The third added explicit "NO" scripts. It took eleven iterations across multiple weeks before the chatbot could give a clean answer without adding drift at the end. Budget for more passes than you think you need. The AI runs twenty-four hours a day. One training pass is not enough.

Step 10: Launch the Keeper Feedback Loop

Encourage all Keepers to report:

- Drift sightings
- Misalignment
- Confusing language
- Outdated expectations
- Questionable claims
- Unstable AI behavior

Outcome: Feedback becomes fuel for ongoing truth alignment.

The Day 90 Goal

By day 90, your company will:

- Speak with one truth
- Eliminate legacy promises
- Catch drift early
- Correct inconsistencies quickly
- Reduce customer confusion
- Reduce team rework
- Stabilize onboarding
- Align human and AI representatives
- Improve accuracy across channels
- Simplify leadership decisions

- Build operational predictability
- Increase customer trust
- Perform better with fewer surprises

In short: You will operate like a Promise Company.

And once that identity takes root, it changes everything — your culture, your reputation, your performance, your clarity, your ability to scale, your relationship with customers, and your sense of organizational calm.

What Comes After Day 90

PAS isn't a project. It's an operating system.

After Day 90:

- Maintain the Alignment Rhythm
- Continue Weekly Promise Standups
- Run Monthly Stack Reviews
- Conduct Quarterly Gate Calibrations
- Execute Annual Promise Resets

This keeps alignment alive as you grow.

NINE

BUILDING YOUR PROMISE COMPANY

If you've made it this far, you understand something most companies never figure out: **the promises you make—and keep—determine everything.**

Not your vision.

Not your funding.

Not your product roadmap.

Your promises.

Because promises become expectations. Expectations become trust. And trust becomes the foundation for every customer relationship, every employee commitment, and every strategic decision you make.

More importantly, you now understand the real problem: It's not just about over-promising and under-delivering in sales. It's about the systematic breakdown of organizational alignment that creates a customer expectation gap across your entire company. It's about the strategy execution gap where leadership's intentions never translate into consistent customer experiences. It's about the brand promise gap where what you market and what you deliver are fundamentally misaligned.

You've now learned the Promise Alignment System—a framework for ensuring your company says only what it can deliver and delivers exactly what it says. But understanding the system and implementing it are two different things.

This final chapter is about what happens next.

What You've Learned

Let's synthesize what we've covered:

Promise Drift is inevitable—but manageable. As your company grows, promises proliferate through marketing, sales, AI systems, employee improvisation, and legacy content. Without deliberate management, these promises fragment, contradict, and multiply—creating the customer expectation gap that shows up in your NPS scores, churn rates, and support ticket volumes. This is the hidden source of over-promising and under-delivering: not reckless salespeople, but organizational misalignment.

PAS closes the strategy execution gap. The Promise Alignment System doesn't eliminate drift. It catches it. The Core Promise anchors everything. The Stack organizes your commitments. The Gate stops new drift before it spreads. The Alignment Rhythm creates regular checkpoints. The Alignment Network ensures everyone knows what to keep. The Drift Audit surfaces misalignment before customers do. **Together, these tools create organizational alignment around the one thing that matters most: keeping your word.**

The six components work as a system. You can't cherry-pick. The Core Promise without the Gate means you'll still drift. The Stack without the Rhythm means it'll decay. The Drift Audit without the Alignment Network means problems get found but not fixed. These tools reinforce each other— that's what makes PAS work. That's what closes the brand promise gap permanently.

Implementation is messy. Remember AxisLine's journey in Part 1. Their AI hallucinated for weeks. Sales rebelled against the Gate. The first Stack Review was a disaster. It took six months to see real transformation, not six weeks. Your journey will be messy too. That's normal.

But transformation is real. When AxisLine finally aligned, everything changed. NPS climbed. Teams relaxed. Customers trusted them. Leaders made decisions faster. The offshore team stopped guessing. They became the company that keeps its word—and that became their competitive advantage.

You can do the same.

Why Closing the Expectation Gap Matters More Than Ever

The world has changed in ways that make the cost of over-promising and under-delivering higher than ever:

The strategy execution gap is now exponential. AI makes promise proliferation automatic. Your chatbots, automated emails, and AI-generated content are making promises right now—possibly contradicting your actual capabilities. What used to be a gap between leadership and frontline teams is now a gap between leadership and autonomous systems that generate responses 24/7 without human oversight.

Customers have zero tolerance for the brand promise gap. They've been burned too many times by companies that overpromise and underdeliver. Today, trust is the scarcest resource in business. Customers will forgive a company that's slow or expensive—but they won't forgive a company that lies, even accidentally. **Your brand promise must match customer experience, or you'll lose them forever.**

Organizational alignment is your only competitive advantage. In a market flooded with noise, hype, and empty promises, the companies that win are the ones that do exactly what they say they'll do. Not the fastest. Not the flashiest. The most reliable. **The ones that have closed the customer expectation gap and can prove it.**

Distributed teams amplify every misalignment. When your team is spread across time zones, offices, and continents, the strategy execution gap becomes exponentially harder to close. Your offshore team in Manila operates on different assumptions than your sales team in Austin. Your contractors use outdated documentation. Your agencies create messages you never approved. Without organizational alignment around promises, distributed work creates distributed drift.

Your culture depends on closing the gap. When employees constantly apologize for promises they didn't make or scramble to deliver outcomes they can't control, they burn out. When leaders make decisions based on conflicting information, they lose credibility. When systems contradict each other, frustration becomes the default. **Promise alignment isn't just about**

customers—it's about building a culture where people can succeed because everyone is working toward the same commitments.

This is why Promise Companies will dominate the next decade. Not because they're perfect—but because they've eliminated the customer expectation gap that destroys trust.

The Choice: Continue Over-Promising, or Close the Gap

You're standing at a decision point.

Option 1: Accept the customer expectation gap as inevitable. Let promises drift. Hope marketing and delivery stay aligned. Trust that your offshore team knows what customers were told. Assume your AI is generating accurate responses. Keep over-promising and under-delivering because "that's just how business works." Put out fires as they arise. Grow chaotically.

Most companies choose this path. It's easier in the short term. No new meetings. No new processes. No pushback from teams who don't want to change.

But you already know where this leads. The strategy execution gap widens. The brand promise gap erodes trust. Customer churn increases. Employees burn out. Competitors who've achieved organizational alignment start taking your market share.

Option 2: Choose alignment. Close the gap. Define your Core Promise. Build your Stack. Install the Gate. Implement the Rhythm. Train your Alignment Network. Run the Drift Audit. Do the hard work of becoming a Promise Company—one that has permanently closed the customer expectation gap between what you say and what you do.

This path is harder in the short term. There will be resistance. Sales will push back on the Gate. Teams will complain about "more meetings." Some promises you love will fail the feasibility test.

But you also know where this leads. You saw it in AxisLine's transformation. **The strategy execution gap closes. Over-promising and under-delivering stops. The brand promise aligns with customer experience.** NPS climbs.

Teams relax. Customers trust you. Leaders make decisions faster. Culture improves. Growth becomes sustainable instead of chaotic.

The choice is yours.

But understand this: **not choosing is a choice.** If you close this book and do nothing, you've chosen Option 1. The customer expectation gap will continue to widen. The gap between what you promise and what you deliver will grow. And eventually, customers will stop believing you—or worse, they'll stop caring.

Your First Three Actions

If you're ready to choose alignment, here's what to do in the next 30 days:

Action 1: Define Your Core Promise (This Week)

Don't overthink it. Gather your leadership team. Use the Core Promise Formula from Chapter 1:

"We [specific outcome] for [target customer] [frequency/consistency qualifier]."

Start with what you actually deliver consistently today—not what you aspire to deliver someday. Test it against the "heroics test": Can you deliver this promise even on your worst day, with your worst-performing team member, for your most difficult customer?

If no, simplify it until the answer is yes.

Deliverable: One sentence. Written down. Shared with leadership. This becomes your North Star.

Action 2: Run Your First
Drift Audit (Within 30 Days)

Don't wait to build the perfect Stack or install the Gate. Start by finding out what promises you're actually making right now.

Gather everything:

- Your website (all pages)
- Marketing materials
- Sales decks and proposals
- Onboarding docs
- Support knowledge base
- AI chatbot conversation logs
- Automated email sequences
- Legacy documentation
- Offshore team training materials

Compare every promise against your Core Promise. Ask: Does this align? Does this contradict? Do we actually deliver this?

You'll be shocked at what you find.

Deliverable: A list of every promise you're making, sorted by alignment status. You don't need to fix everything immediately—just know what you're working with.

Action 3: Install the Promise
Gate (Within 60 Days)

Create a simple intake process for new promises. Before anyone in your company makes a new promise—in marketing, sales, product, or anywhere else—it goes through the Gate.

Start with just the three Gate Questions:

1. CAN we deliver this? (Capability)
2. SHOULD we deliver this? (Alignment with Core Promise)

     BUILDING YOUR PROMISE COMPANY

3. WILL we deliver this? (Resource commitment)

Don't make it complicated. A simple form. A 15-minute review meeting. A clear yes/no decision.

Deliverable: A functional Promise Gate with at least one decision logged. Even if it's imperfect, it's operational.

The Invitation

You're now equipped to build a Promise Company.

The framework is clear. The tools are defined. The roadmap is in front of you. But frameworks don't transform companies—**leaders do.**

Leaders who care enough to define what they stand for.

Leaders who are brave enough to say no to promises they can't keep.

Leaders who are humble enough to admit when they've drifted.

Leaders who are disciplined enough to install systems that prevent future drift.

Are you that leader?

If yes, the work starts now. Not next quarter. Not after the next product launch. Not when things "settle down." Now.

Because every day you wait, your company makes more promises. Your customers form more expectations. Your teams commit to more outcomes. Your AI generates more responses. Your drift compounds.

But every day you practice alignment, you build more trust. Your customers feel more confident. Your teams feel more supported. Your culture gets stronger. Your competitive advantage grows.

One Final Truth

The work never ends. Drift is gravity—it's always pulling. But gravity doesn't make you fall. Gravity just means you have to stand deliberately.

PAS gives you a way to stand.

The Core Promise keeps you grounded. The Stack keeps you organized. The Gate keeps you protected. The rhythm keeps you consistent. The Network keeps you supported. The Audit keeps you honest.

Together, they create something powerful: **a company that keeps its word.**

Not sometimes. Not mostly. Not when it's convenient.

Every time.

That's what Promise Companies do. And that's what you're capable of becoming.

Ready to Begin?

Let's get started on your promise alignment.

The framework is here. The roadmap is clear. Whatever support you need—diagnostics, tools, or guidance—you'll find it at **promisealignment.com**.

The choice is yours. ***Will you build a Promise Company?***

ACKNOWLEDGMENTS

This book would not have been possible without the help of thoughtful leaders that I trusted to bring this to life.

Liam, Meredith, Kelly and Chelsea - thank you for encouraging me and taking the time to read through my early concepts and challenging me.

To those that have shaped my professional perspective and given me opportunities to come alongside you - thank you.

ABOUT THE AUTHOR

Arturo Coto is a founder, CEO, and operator with 30 years of experience across market research, management consulting, technology, mobile payments, and retail.

Throughout his career, Arturo consistently focused on a core organizational challenge: how companies define, communicate, and govern the promises they make — to customers, partners, and internal teams. Across growth-stage and enterprise environments, he observed that many execution failures, delivery risks, and internal breakdowns were not the result of poor strategy or insufficient capability, but of misaligned and unmanaged commitments.

Over time, this observation evolved into a structured point of view: that promises themselves represent a distinct and governable unit of organizational risk. This perspective became the foundation for both this book and the **Promise Alignment System**.

arturocoto.com